The Dynamics of
Corporate Worship

Other books in the
Ministry Dynamics for a New Century series
Warren W. Wiersbe, series editor

Also by Vernon M. Whaley

Books

Music Publications

The Dynamics of
Corporate
Worship

VERNON M. WHALEY

BakerBooks
A Division of Baker Book House Co
Grand Rapids, Michigan 49516

Published by Baker Books
a division of Baker Book House Company
P.O. Box 6287, Grand Rapids, MI 49516-6287

Printed in the United States of America

Library of Congress Cataloging-in-Publication Data

Whaley, Vernon M., 1949–
   The dynamics of corporate worship / Vernon M. Whaley.
       p.   cm.—(Ministry dynamics for a new century)
   Includes bibliographical references.
   ISBN 0-8010-9109-8 (pbk.)
   1. Public worship. I. Series.
BV15.W44   2001
264—dc21   00-051922

The song "Everything I Have Is Praise" in chapter 10 is by Kenn Mann, © 2000 by Lorenz Publishing Company, P.O. Box 802, Dayton, OH 45401-0802. All rights reserved. Used by permission.

Unless otherwise indicated, Scripture quotations are from the HOLY BIBLE, NEW INTERNATIONAL VERSION®. NIV®. Copyright © 1973, 1978, 1984 by International Bible Society. Used by permission of Zondervan Publishing House. All rights reserved.

Scripture quotations identified KJV are from the King James Version of the Bible.

Scripture quotations identified NKJV are from the New King James Version. Copyright © 1979, 1980, 1982 by Thomas Nelson, Inc. Used by permission. All rights reserved.

For current information about all releases from Baker Book House, visit our web site:
http://www.bakerbooks.com

To
my wonderful Lord and sovereign King, Jesus Christ,
who is worthy of all honor, glory, and praise,
and to
Etheline P. Whaley,
my mother, friend, prayer partner,
and fellow worshiper
(who went to be with the Lord on June 5, 2000,
during the writing of this book)
for encouraging me to tell the story
of corporate worship

Contents

Series Preface

The purpose of the Ministry Dynamics series is to provide both experienced and beginning pastors with concise information that will help them do the task of ministry with efficiency, fruitfulness, and joy.

The word *ministry* means "service," something that Jesus exemplified in his own life and that he expects us to practice in our lives. No matter what our title or position, we are in the church to serve God's people. The word *dynamics* is not used as an equivalent of "power" but as a reminder that nothing stands still in Christian ministry. If it does, it dies. True biblical ministry involves constant challenge and change, learning and growth, and how we handle these various elements determines the strength and success of the work that we do.

The emphasis in this series is on practical service founded on basic principles and not on passing fads. Some older ministers need to catch up with the present, while newer ministers need to catch up on the past. We all can learn much from each other if only we're honest enough to admit it and humble enough to accept each other's counsel.

I began pastoring in 1950 and over the years have seen many changes take place in local church ministry, from bus ministries and house churches to growth groups and megachurches. Some of the changes have been good and are now integrated into God's work in many churches. But some ideas that attracted national attention decades ago now exist only on the pages of forgotten books in used-book stores. How quickly today's exciting headlines become tomorrow's footnotes! "Test everything. Hold on to the good" (1 Thess. 5:21).

An ancient anonymous prayer comes to mind:

> From the cowardice that shrinks from new truth,
> From the laziness that is content with half-truths,
> From the arrogance that thinks it knows all truth,
>   O God of truth, deliver us!

Our desire is that both the seasoned servant and the new seminary graduate will find encouragement and enlightenment from the Ministry Dynamics series.

Warren W. Wiersbe

Acknowledgments

I wish to thank the following for contributing to the processes of this book:

Beth S. Whaley—my wife, friend, and companion for twenty-eight years—for loving me no matter the circumstances and for challenging me to capture the vision of walking with God through daily worship.

Warren Wiersbe—for asking me to be part of his book series. He is an encourager who knows how to worship!

Don Stephenson and the editors at Baker Books—for patience and guidance in finishing the manuscript. They are the best!

Jonathan Thigpen, my friend and fellow soldier—for urging me to accept the opportunity to write this book.

Joe Grizzle—for teaching me the joy of lifestyle worship.

Rob Morgan—for being the first to share with me the truth about worship from Matthew 28:16–20.

Melvin Worthington—for teaching me how to study the Bible for preaching.

Jack Williams—friend, encourager, writer, editor, and author—for teaching me to value the wonder and power of the written Word.

Jim Colman, chairman, department of music, and the students at Cedarville University—for giving me a place to try out my ideas.

Don Wyrtzen—for being the other partner and team member committed to practicing and teaching worship.

Janet Wells, Jack and Christine Daniel—for proofreading portions of the text.

Dr. Ted Traylor, pastor, Olive Baptist Church, Pensacola, Florida—for loving our family and giving me the wonderful opportunity to practice corporate worship and in the process becoming a trusted friend.

Liberty Heights Church, Pisgah Heights, Ohio, Dr. Terry Fields, pastor; and the Far Hills Baptist Church, Dayton, Ohio, Dr. John Jackson, pastor—for giving me the honor and opportunity of practicing corporate worship on a weekly basis.

Introduction

A large crowd gathers for Thursday night worship. The building is a convincing structure that looks more like a Broadway theater than what most would call a worship center. The impressive lighting, television monitors, wonderful decor, accent art, staging, and state-of-the-art sound system all serve as imposing reminders that this is no ordinary gathering of worship leaders. The lights dim. An intense hush settles over the crowd. A band plays praise and worship songs with energy and purpose. The curtain rises. A worship leader proclaims in a loud voice, "Let the body of Christ worship the living Lord." The members of the congregation spontaneously leap to their feet, begin to clap to the rhythm of the music, and instantly engage in worship. The gospel is presented in drama, video, personal testimony, song, and preaching—Jesus is glorified, and they worship!

Five thousand miles to the northwest, a small group gathers in a building on the Alaskan tundra. It's already cold and dark outside, but inside the group meets in sweet fellowship and love for each other. It's the only church in this village of nearly two hundred mostly Alaskan Indians. The service is quiet and subdued—no piano, no sound system, no video. The building doesn't even have electricity. The music is simple and accompanied by guitar. Believers spontaneously share testimonies of praise and rejoice in the goodness of God. A former alcoholic reads Scripture. A former prostitute lifts up holy hands to the Lord. They listen and feed on the Word as a young pastor preaches—and they worship!

Family members gather around the bed of a dying saint. Their dad, husband, and brother is dying of a blood disorder. In a matter of moments he will pass from this life to the next. The family is facing the reality of death and the certainty of eternity. A family member reads Scripture. All day, they share with each other the joy of family. They pray for a swift and painless home going. They praise God together. Even Dad joins as they sing the refrain of a hymn. Then he closes his eyes and slips into eternity. The family joins hands and spontaneously sings "God Is So Good" and "I Love You, Lord"—and they worship!

Unseasonably warm October sunshine makes its way through the one-hundred-year-old stained glass windows. With power and majesty, the organist plays "A Mighty Fortress Is Our God" on the old pipe organ. The congregation joins the choir in singing "How Firm a Foundation." The banner ministry presents the names of Jehovah on cue while the choir sings "No Other Name but the Name of Jesus." The preaching is characterized by its impeccable theology, sprinkled with practical application. The wonders of God are proclaimed. The body of Christ celebrates communion—and they worship.

The service begins with the energetic, a cappella singing of an enthusiastic African-American gospel choir. They *know* how to sing gospel. Congregational singing continues for nearly forty-five minutes. A soloist sings of the glory of God. A Hammond B-3 organ fills the room with music. People shout praises to God. The preacher presents the gospel with power and conviction. The congregation gives glory to the Lord—and they worship!

Thus is the dynamic of corporate worship—people of diverse and broad cultural backgrounds, life experiences, and personal preferences declaring genuine love and devotion to God, together! You see, there is nothing magical about the time for worship, building, style of music, number of worship leaders, drama, pipe organ, use of elaborate and sophisticated graphics software, stained glass, or chosen method of singing and preaching. What makes biblical worship dynamic is that it emerges out of a genuine hunger to know and express love for God together—in one mind, in one accord. Such worship begins in the hearts of many individuals and is expressed to God collectively. The optimal word is *together*. So why then is the body of Christ engaged in a war over worship?

Since accepting the challenge of writing this book, I've watched with great interest how much we fuss and fight over issues surrounding corporate worship. I thought when I began this journey that the intensity of disagreements regarding worship was beginning to ease. In fact, I even questioned the need for another book on worship. But the issues surrounding worship continue to swirl in controversy. Worship wars are raging and wounded soldiers are scattered along both sides of a highway called biblical worship. Disagreements over worship preferences, traditions, style and choice of music, cultural identity, and much more form the platform for controversy. The very thing that should draw the body of Christ together—worship of Jehovah God—has become a source of deep and damaging division.

Satan is well aware that worship of Jehovah is at the heart of our relationship with God. As the evil one, he does everything in his power to distract and disrupt genuine praise flowing to the throne of God. Historically, he has been most successful at getting God's people to argue and fuss about worship. He is successful at getting those of us who worship Christ so captivated and caught up in arguments about worship that we don't spend time worshiping and enjoying God.

This book is a practical guide to understanding the principles of corporate worship. It is not an exhaustive treatise on the theology of worship nor a how-to fix-all for doing worship. I have deliberately tried to stay away from developing a treatise on worship styles and practices common to the evangelical community.

It might be helpful for you to view this book in three sections. Chapters 1 to 3 discuss the dynamic elements of corporate worship. I am persuaded that a person must enjoy meaningful worship in his or her private life before God will bless that person with the joy of success in public worship. Thus, three chapters deal with worship on a personal level. Chapters 4 to 6 are about dynamic examples in corporate worship. In this section I have provided a brief history of worship from Genesis 1 through Revelation, an overview of the relationship of worship to the great awakenings and revivals, and a biblical foundation for worship as outlined in Psalm 96. The third section contains dynamic essentials for corporate worship. The five principles for worship presented in chapter 6 serve as the foundation for chapters 7 to 12—two chapters on worship and music and one chapter each devoted to evangelism, giving, prayer, and preaching. Chapters 13, 14, and 15 deal with the more pragmatic side of corporate worship, including principles for working with people, serving, and keeping services practical. As with much of the book, the last three chapters are gleaned from personal experiences.

I trust this volume will enable people to better focus on God and better equip God's people to worship in spirit and in truth. It is my heart's desire that the experiences and truths about corporate worship shared here will burn in your heart and ignite a flame of passion to know God in all his glory and that your congregation will worship him with freedom, conviction, and joy.

One

The Dynamics of Honest Worship

> The sacrifices of God are a broken spirit; a broken and contrite heart.
>
> Psalm 51:17

The room was dingy and unusually dirty. The smell of old grease and overcooked french fries cast a spell over the entire building. The Oklahoma sun crept through the smudged and dirty windows of the old BBQ restaurant and landed right across the man's face. I sat spellbound as he methodically and graciously told me about the Sunday morning church services at his church.

"We meet from 10:30 to noon on Sundays," he said.

"Wow!" I replied. "How much music?"

"We usually have about twenty minutes of worship and praise choruses mixed with a few hymns."

I thought, *Oh, brother, this guy preaches for an hour and ten minutes.* "So," I said, "how much time do you devote to the preaching?"

"Oh, about twenty minutes."

"So what do you do with the rest of the time?"

His eyes betrayed an obvious struggle to restrain deep emotions. "Well, Vernon, we pray."

"You do what?" I said.

"We pray."

The purpose of this meeting was to talk about his church. This pastor had asked me to consider coming to his church of about two hundred to serve as minister of music and worship. Immediately, I had declined the invitation by citing a need for a career change. He had persisted. I had continued to decline. Finally, he asked if he could take me to lunch and tell me how the Lord was teaching his church about worship.

For better than an hour, this pastor and friend told me how the Lord led him to an understanding of worship and praise. I listened, convicted of my own neglect of worship and strangely troubled by this man's open, honest, and forthright approach to meeting God on a daily basis. He told how he leads his church in times of extended public prayer during the morning service. Each Sunday morning service, this brother walks down from the pulpit area and into the congregation. He writes down prayer requests on a notepad as they are shared—one by one—by the people. He then asks everyone to stand, join hands, and pray. After about fifteen minutes of simply praising and worshiping God as lord, creator, redeemer, provider, healer, and sustainer, he leads his people in a concentrated time of intercessory prayer—sometimes lasting up to thirty minutes. The entire congregation spontaneously and joyously concludes the time by singing a chorus or the verse of a hymn.

I sat amazed and in wonder as he told how the church had split on the second Sunday of his tenure as pastor. In good faith he had moved his family from California to Oklahoma, unaware of any problem. After the split he was left to pastor a group of emotionally hurt and spiritually wounded believers. One by one, family by family, this brother won and discipled people into the church. Some years later, the Lord laid on his heart the need to spend an hour a day in private prayer. As he learned to pray, he also practiced praising God. The more he praised, the more God blessed. The Sunday worship service was an outgrowth of his private worship. He preached from an overflow found only on his knees. The church began to grow. People, once alienated by anger, harsh words, and bitterness, were now full of joy.

Honest Worship Involves an Honest Evaluation of Love for God

At the time of my lunch with this pastor, I had devoted better than fifteen years of my life to planning, preparing, and providing music for worship. But seldom had I led God's people in genuine worship. I could sing "My Jesus, I Love Thee," "It Is Well with My Soul," and "Trust and Obey" with the most experienced and traditional evangelical. It was natural for me to rally people together with a rousing gospel song. I was gifted at exciting people of God while enthusiastically singing a majestic hymn. I was skilled at leading large choirs in great and exciting gospel songs, expressing enthusiasm about the love of God, and providing music with excellence and professional skill. But my heart was full of pride. I harbored bitterness toward brothers in Christ. Anger in my heart often flared up toward those in authority. I was bound by legalism. While I could lead people in music at rousing and exciting revival services, rarely did I lead God's people to the throne of grace in true, genuine worship. The reality: God had to change my heart.

I believe I was like most of us who call ourselves evangelical: We sneer at the traditional church, calling them liberal and too formal. We look at their emphasis on liturgy with the smugness of a Pharisee and say to God,

"Thank you that I'm not like that." We talk about our need for warm, personal, congregational worship, but rarely do we worship. We preach sermons on prayer but spend little time in corporate prayer. We stand in our pulpits and encourage our congregations to praise God but allow little time for praise. We write volumes of books on the style and manner of worship. Still, we don't worship much. As ministers and musicians, we invent persuasive arguments as to why we should be spontaneous, hang on to the old songs, introduce the new, or develop a blended approach to worship. We lecture on the need to worship, God's plan for worship, why God made us to worship, and that everyone will worship in eternity—and still, we do very little worshiping.

Charles C. Ryrie provides for us an exceptional, concise, and academically profound definition of worship:

> The worship of the church, then, consists of individual, corporate, public, and private service for the Lord which is generated by a reverence for and submission to Him who is totally worthy.[1]

Indeed, the English word *worship* is actually a shortened form of the word *worthship*. The word implies that one should attribute worth to an object worshiped. It comes from the Greek word *Proskuneo,* meaning to prostrate oneself in reverence. It is the word Jesus used for worship in John 4:24. May I suggest, however, that there is more, much more to worship. Worship is more than service, more than reverence, more than submission. Worship, yea, even corporate worship, is seeing God as God, loving genuinely, adoring affectionately. In A. W. Tozer's words:

> Worship is to feel in the heart. . . . Real worship is, among other things, a feeling about the Lord our God. . . . If we are led by His Holy Spirit, our wor-

ship will always bring a delighted sense of admiring awe and a sincere humility on our part.[2]

Honest Worship Involves an Honest Expression of Love to God

So how does one worship honestly? How does one experience corporate worship that is both dynamic and delightful?

First, to worship, we must come to God with a broken spirit. The broken and contrite heart is essential to biblical worship. The psalmist characterized it this way: "You do not delight in sacrifice, or I would bring it; you do not take pleasure in burnt offerings. The sacrifices of God are a broken spirit; a broken and a contrite heart, O God, you will not despise" (Ps. 51:16–17). As a congregation, we should break our commitment to formula worship and the trite habit of meeting for the sake of meeting. As individuals, we must be broken of the pride, arrogance, and selfishness that drives us to serve and to be "righteous" performers.

Second, if we are going to be worshipers, we must practice worshiping. Bob MacKenzie is a Nashville record producer and friend. In recent years, Bob has been involved in producing and recording black gospel choirs in Los Angeles. Upon returning from a recent visit to Los Angeles and recording one of the fabulous mass choirs there, Bob said, "Do you know, Vernon, what the biggest difference is between white and black gospel choirs? Most white folks go to choir rehearsal to practice music for worship. These African-American brothers and sisters worship as they practice their music." The reality: Worship must be practiced. A marathon runner is never successful without rigorous training and consistent practice. The concert musician is not successful until he or she falls in love with the practice room. The basketball star only rises to the occasion after hours rehearsing plays and throwing the ball through the hoop. Likewise, worship must be practiced. We will fail miserably in our worship if we wait until a church service to focus on God. Our praise to God should be continual (Heb. 13:15). The psalmist proclaims, "I will extol the LORD at all times" (Ps. 34:1). Corporate worship should be the gathering of believers who are already involved in the practice of praise.

Third, God is more interested in us knowing him than in our commitment to form, tradition, a particular style of worship music, or established ecclesiastical norms. Jesus rebuked the Pharisees because they were more interested in form and ritual than in cultivating a relationship with the living God. There is something to be said about the Christian who has never lost the wonder of salvation, the wonder of redemption, and the wonder of God. That is what the apostle Paul meant when he said "that I may know him, and the power of his resurrection, and the fellowship of his sufferings" (Phil. 3:10 KJV).

Fourth, our public worship must be an outgrowth of our private time with God. How can we please God in worship on Sunday if we live according to the rules of this carnal world during the week? How can we hope to worship God in spirit and in truth as a congregation when the sanctuary of our heart is crowded by busyness, pride, and selfish thoughts? A. W. Tozer put it this way:

> If you do not know the presence of God in your office, your factory, your home, then God is not in the church when you attend. I have come to believe that when we are worshipping—if the love of God is in us and the Spirit of God is breathing praise within us, all the musical instruments in heaven are suddenly playing in full support. . . . It is my experience that our total lives, our entire attitude as persons, must be toward the worship of God.[3]

Honest Worship Involves an Honest Expectation of Love from God

My wife and I accepted the pastor's invitation to minister at the church in Norman, Oklahoma. Our ministry with this dear pastor turned out to be some of the most refreshing and fulfilling years of our marriage, and we stayed during the better part of our children's teenage years. This wonderful pastor never finished college, never pastored a church of thousands, and never sought recognition by his denomination. But he spoke with passion and authority. He had something few men understand or possess—a heart for God.

I believe the church's commitment to private and corporate worship had an eternal impact on our lives. My ministry took on a new and deeper dimension. Genuine love and devotion for God and his people replaced bitterness in my life. We watched and marveled as God used corporate worship to nurture our wounded hearts. We witnessed God working as he developed young Christians, mended crushed lives, rebuilt broken homes, and brought the backslidden into renewed, fresh fellowship with him. The pastor's secret? He understood and practiced honest worship. He in turn taught his congregation to worship honestly.

At the heart of successful and dynamic worship, private or public, is the issue of being honest with God and ourselves. We must honestly evaluate our love for God, genuinely express love to God, and sincerely expect love from God. I am amazed that God still seeks those who worship him in spirit and in truth. Our corporate worship must grow out of an intense desire to know and love God in all his fullness.

Two
The Dynamics of Genuine Worship

Let us exalt his name together.

Psalm 34:3

A few years ago, friends invited my wife, Beth, and me to a café in Franklin, Tennessee, for a Friday evening dinner. This quaint restaurant features a tasty dinner and some form of country, folk, jazz, or Christian music entertainment. On this particular evening, Buddy Green, featured harmonica player with the Gaither Trio and former guitarist for Jerry Reed, performed with the world famous Dobro player, Jerry Douglas. They sang and played country, blue grass, and gospel music for more than two hours.

It was incredible. They held the audience spellbound with their talents and exceptional musicianship. On several occasions Buddy led the group in praise choruses and hymns. He sang my favorites: "God's Own Lamb," "Mary, Did You Know?" and "I Don't Belong." Near the end of their concert, Buddy sang a new composition about the majesty of God. He sang of God choosing to live within our hearts so that we too can experience his wonder and grace. God was honored. His name was uplifted. We were encouraged and edified. Buddy and Jerry did not make a grand announcement, saying, "It's time to worship." But there in the shuffle of a busy restaurant, they led us in genuine corporate worship.

Characteristics of Genuine Worship

Genuine worship? Doesn't that strike you as somewhat strange terminology? Can real, authentic worship be anything but genuine? Is there a litmus test for genuine corporate worship? How does one know when worship is a sweet-smelling aroma to the Lord?

First, worship is genuine when we exalt the Lord. His name is lifted high. He receives glory. He is honored. He is blessed. He is magnified. He is crowned King. The psalmist wrote, "Glorify the LORD with me; let us exalt his name together" (Ps. 34:3). Again, the psalmist declared, "Exalt him also in the congregation of the people and praise him in the assembly" (Ps. 107:32).

The setting was the chapel of Westminster Choir College. It was the summer of 1980. For the better part of four weeks I studied with the world's best and most talented musicians. On Friday night of each week, the participants from the summer program, graduate and undergraduate students from the college, and hundreds of musicians from the community joined together in presenting a major choral work. On one occasion, we performed J. S. Bach's *St. Matthew's Passion,* led by a special guest conductor and accompanied by a world-class chamber orchestra, organist, and vocal soloists. The congregation was the choir, an impressive group of about 300 professional musicians of one type or another. All in all, about 425 musicians joined together to perform this grand choral masterpiece.

The entire presentation was electrifying. The energy level intensified as the instruments played, soloists sang, and congregational choir performed. The gospel story was told in song. People wept as the glorious text "O sacred head now wounded" moved in time with the music. The orchestra and organ played at full volume, the choir and soloists joined in singing the hallelujahs, and the conductor led with profound passion. We were captured by the moment as we worshiped the risen Lord. That night, we exalted the Savior and participated in corporate worship.

Second, genuine worship of Jehovah edifies the saints. Strange as it may seem, the closer we get to the Lord in worship, the closer we are drawn to one another in Christian love. Corporate worship is a "together" thing. We build up one another when we join together in worship. We edify when we witness, sing and share, confess sins, greet, receive, serve, fellowship, participate in communion, and wash feet—all with one another. Worship is all about serving (see chapter 14). In so doing, we build up and encourage one another.

Third, God's people are encouraged when worship and praise are genuine. When we offer praise to God in worship, we take the spotlight off ourselves. Our attention is drawn away from personality and ego, successes and failures, tranquility and troubles, humility and pride. When we practice worship, we are drawn to the all sufficiency of a loving heavenly Father who meets our needs, fulfills our desires, calms our fears, and grants us peace of heart and mind. We are encouraged.

The apostle Paul talks about this principle of encouragement in 2 Corinthians 9:11: "You will be made rich in every way so that you can be generous on every occasion, and through us your generosity will result in thanksgiving to God." Paul first explains how the Christians at Corinth personally encourage him. It is by their giving that the work of God is sustained. Then, like a stockbroker giving a quarterly report, he explains how their giving, a gesture of love and in itself worship, reaps eternal dividends of encouragement to those giving and receiving: God's grace abounds in their lives (v. 8); the work of God is supported (v. 8); the lives of God's people are enriched (v. 11); they learn to praise God (v. 11); needs are supplied (v. 12); other men and women praise God's name (v. 12); God's work is enlarged and others are blessed (v. 13); people practice praying for one another (v. 14); and God is blessed (v. 15).

Peter encourages the Christians in their sufferings with praise to God: "Blessed be the God and Father of our Lord Jesus Christ, which according to his abundant mercy hath begotten us again unto a lively hope" (1 Peter 1:3 KJV), "the God of all grace, who hath called us unto his eternal glory by Christ Jesus, after that ye have suffered a while, make you perfect, stablish, strengthen, settle you. To him be glory and dominion forever and ever" (1 Peter 5:10–11 KJV). Our dear brother Peter understood first-hand this principle through Jesus' admonition: "In this world you will have trouble. But take heart! I have overcome the world" (John 16:33).

When God's people actively engage in corporate praise and worship, they and the people around them are encouraged. God uses praise to him as a method for building up the lives and ministries of his own.

Fourth, we evangelize when our worship is genuine. In chapter 9, the case for evangelism and worship is presented. People take notice when God does his work. The ungodly stand in wonder as they witness God's work in the hearts of men. They are amazed by God's power to transform broken lives into vessels of service. I love the way Warren Wiersbe describes this process: "No church abandons evangelism . . . when it returns to worship. Rather, it enriches that evangelism and gives it spiritual depth."[1] People take notice when God does his work.

Fifth, the Holy Spirit uses genuine worship and praise as means for exhorting us to greater service. At the heart of worship is the spirit of serving—serving others while serving Christ. Quoting Warren Wiersbe:

> The more we minister to one another in our daily lives, the easier it will be to minister to one another when we gather to worship God. What is important is that we have the "servant attitude" as we gather. We have not met "to be served, but to serve" (Matt. 20:28).[2]

Sixth, our education about the Sovereign grows through genuine worship—God reveals himself to us in a personal and delightful manner. The disciples were "all with one accord in one place" when God filled the house in the form of a mighty rushing wind (Acts 2). The Holy Spirit was revealed to them as they searched the Scripture. The Sovereign taught them as they focused on him.

Most of us develop friendships as we spend time with people. We learn about their personalities, work ethic, and abilities. We grow in friendship as we spend quality time together. So it is with God. A congregation learns more about one another, about God, and about his church as they worship together. Consider this: Abraham of old learned about God's provisions when he worshiped (Genesis 18). Jacob learned about God's presence as he worshiped (Genesis 28). It was in the damp of a dirty prison that Joseph learned about God's providence (Genesis 39–45). Job learned the truth of Jehovah-Rohi, the healer, and worshiped (Job 42). It was after Joshua and God's people worshiped outside the walls of Jericho that they learned about Jehovah-Nissi, the God of victory (Joshua 6). Isaiah experienced God's cleansing through worship (Isaiah 6). Amos learned about God's judgment when witnessing false worship (Amos 4:4–13). The disciples learned about worship through the Lord's Prayer (Matthew 6). It was as Paul and Silas worshiped that they learned about God's salvation to a Philippian jailer (Acts 16). The church "prayed without ceasing" for Peter and learned about the power of God to deliver (Acts 12). John the Revelator learned about the principles of praise as he saw thousands from every tribe and nation worshiping around the throne proclaiming, "Worthy is the Lamb that was slain . . . blessing, and honor, and glory, and power be unto him that sitteth upon the throne, and unto the Lamb forever and ever" (Rev. 5:12–13 KJV).

Seventh, our vision of God and his church is enlarged as we practice genuine worship and praise. The Bible records the prophet Isaiah seeing the Lord high and lifted up. As the prophet saw the truth of God's holiness, conviction of sin and an awareness of the Almighty One's awesome presence captured his attention. It was then he heard "the voice of the Lord, saying, Whom shall I send, and who will go for us? Then said I, Here am I; send me" (Isa. 6:8 KJV). Our vision of God's church is enlarged when we worship.

We can learn from our dear brother Isaiah. He did not commit himself to tradition. His commitment was not to a form of worship. He did not confine worship of the almighty Jehovah God to his own culture or meeting place. Isaiah did not seek to squeeze worship into his own preferred style of preaching or singing. No. His commitment to God rose above the things we often label as true worship: the sermon, order of worship, music, choir renderings, special music, offertory, entrance, proclamations of grace, and the other things we choose to include in our worship structure. Isaiah's commitment was to God alone. As a result of seeing God "high and lifted up," Isaiah saw his own life, family, nation, even the work of the ministry as a part of the whole. God enlarged his vision.

The Calling to Genuine Worship

About fifteen years ago in Kansas City I experienced a remarkable week. More than 250 of us joined together for the International Choral Music Festival hosted by the University of Missouri at Kansas City Conservatory of Music. One of the participants of the festival was a doctorate student at the conservatory and a member of a large African Methodist Episcopal Church in Kansas City. Because he was choir director at the church, the pastor granted him permission to invite the entire group to sing at the church on Sunday morning. Our group included educators and choral directors from a variety of ethnic and religious backgrounds—saved and unsaved—Presbyterian, Methodist, Christian Missionary Alliance, Baptist (of all kinds), charismatic, Lutheran, a New Ager or two, an agnostic, and more, all together in one place on a bright August Sunday morning. We prepared "How Lovely Is Thy Dwelling" from the Brahms Requiem and Gilbert Martin's arrangement of "When I Survey the Wondrous Cross."

The service began promptly at 10:00 A.M. The church choir processed from the back of the sanctuary singing, "Praise him, praise him, praise him in the morning, praise him at the noontime, praise him, praise him, praise him when the sun goes down." The congregation stood and sang for nearly forty minutes. We started with "All Hail the Power of Jesus' Name" and the doxology and continued with Dottie Rambo's "Lift Him Up" and Andre Crouch's "Bless the Lord, O My Soul." It was a glorious time as we sang familiar and unfamiliar songs with conviction and focus. At times I felt as though nobody else was in the building. I was most impressed at how the music director, playing the church pipe organ, moved from song to song and led us as one great crowd of worshipers, never saying a word. There we were, 250 choral directors—many of whom I'm sure did not profess the name of Jesus—held spellbound as a gifted worship leader led God's people to proclaim the wonders of God through song.

About forty-five minutes into the service, the pastor introduced his music director, who in turn welcomed us from the choral festival. He explained to the congregation that we were a group of "professional choral directors" who had prepared music for worship. At that, we stood and sang "How Lovely Is Thy Dwelling." It is exceptionally beautiful, but that morning, the choral masterpiece was particularly stunning. When we finished, the congregation sat in total silence. Then we sang "When I Survey the Wondrous Cross." Never before or since that day have I sung in an ensemble that sang the old hymn with such passion. The sheer sound of 250 voices singing choral literature was breathtaking. The power of the vocal ensemble was most intense and obvious when the choir sang:

Were the whole realm of nature mine,
That were a present far too small:
Love so amazing, so divine,
Demands my soul, my life, my all.

The congregation rose to their feet in thunderous applause when we got to the words "love so amazing, so divine." We finished the song, and they continued to applaud. The pastor asked if we would sing it again. We accommodated. This time, the congregation spontaneously sang the phrase "love so amazing" right along with the choir. Again they responded in glorious applause. I looked over at the tenor on my left and tears were streaming down his face. I glanced over to the women in the section to my right, and they were overcome with emotion. The entire congregation stood and applauded for what seemed like hours in absolute wonder of the moment.

We experienced genuine worship that day in Kansas City. We experienced corporate worship—together. God was exalted and his name was lifted high. Saints were edified and encouraged. Unsaved people witnessed the wonders of God, and Christians were exhorted to greater service. Our knowledge of and vision for God and his church were enlarged.

In reflecting on the event today, I am persuaded that I was captured by the wonder of our almighty, sovereign God. The sheer beauty of his love for humanity—for me—brought me to a genuine place of worship. I witnessed believers answer the calling within their heart of hearts. Unbelievers may not have fully understood what God was doing, but it was obvious that they too knew God was doing something special in the hearts of his people.

What can be said in conclusion about genuine worship? Corporate worship becomes genuine only as our expression of love for God is nurtured in the individual heart—transcends the pressures of culture, peer acceptance, and ecclesiastical nuances—and effortlessly moves beyond the boundaries of evangelical traditions to the place where we meet each week.

Three

The Dynamics of Hindered Worship

> For the LORD seeth not as man seeth. . . . The LORD
> looketh on the heart.
>
> 1 Samuel 16:7 KJV

A couple of years ago, my wife and I were privileged to attend a conference on marriage in Pensacola, Florida, taught by a well-known author and speaker. More than four thousand people gathered in the sanctuary of a large church and listened as the speaker shared principles for successful, happy marriages. Near the conclusion of the second session, he asked each of us to bow our heads and pray. It was the most tender and heart-searching moment of the evening. Hundreds wept as he prayed, asking God to help us love and be committed to the mate God had given us. Almost immediately, however, his prayer was interrupted with a series of uncontrollable sneezes—right into the microphone. All across the auditorium people began snickering. The speaker, in a moment of frustration, quickly said, "Lord, I didn't mean to sneeze, and I guess that's all for tonight." He abruptly walked off the platform, and the service was dismissed. At the moment, it certainly seemed the sneezes had hindered the flow of the service. I am sure that some considered the service a grand flop. But not God. The Holy Spirit used that service to prompt people to obedience. At the very next gathering, hundreds responded during the invitation to the moving of God in their lives.

I'm sure all of us have stories about how well-planned, well-executed worship services have been interrupted and seemingly demolished by circumstances beyond our control—the loud scream of an ambulance during a quiet, sensitive moment; a failed sound system; a glitch in the electronic piano; miscued sound tracks; power failure; problems with an overhead display; people visiting and talking during the service; inappropriate selection of songs for the moment; the occasional sneeze; and, of course, crying babies. Actually, I'm certain each of us can compile our own list of ways to hinder worship. And I'm equally sure we can take each problem and find a nifty solution—at least until it's time to work with people.

It's true, the enemy uses any variety of external circumstances to distract God's children as they seek to worship. It is my observation, however, that the deeper, more profound hindrances to worship are those we usually don't include on a list of external do's and don'ts for worship.

I believe Christians of all generations face common problems related to hindered worship. These are not external circumstances that create an atmosphere for interrupted worship. Rather, they are internal issues that hinder the flow of worship from humans, who desire to worship, to a sovereign God, who alone is worthy of glory, honor, and praise.

Seven Hindrances to Worship

What follows is a list of seven *isms* that characterize hindered worship. I am deliberately using vague terminology to describe general concepts, defining these words in the context of the subject. I realize that some of these terms may have a completely different meaning when applied to philosophy, aesthetics, politics, education, and psychology. In some cases, my terminology may be based on made-up words used to define a broad principle.

The seven internal hindrances to worship are:

1. intellectualism
2. idealism
3. imperialism
4. isolationism
5. institutionalism
6. improperism
7. illusionism

These isms are crippling diseases infecting the body of Christ. Left unchecked, they render corporate worship ineffective. Scripture condemns each ism, which comes from an ego-centered desire to control the outcome of corporate worship.

Intellectualism

The first hindrance to worship is *intellectualism*. This is the doctrine that knowledge comes from pure reason, without aid from the senses. It is also known as rationalism. People with this concept of worship are consumed by all that goes into formulating the definition of the term *worship*. The intellectualist takes what God has intended to be an emotional and spiritual experience and turns it into a mental exercise. Intellectual worship often relates the worship experience to some biblical position of God's worth. Brothers and sisters practicing this kind of worship intellectualize the practice surrounding expressions of love to the Lord. To the intellectual worshiper, every aspect of corporate gatherings is rationalized, evaluated, reconsidered, and analyzed: the form, music, Scripture reading, prayer, and preaching. This worshiper evaluates the purpose, process, and implications involved in every aspect of worship. Elements of worship are ignored, deemphasized, and explained away if for some reason they are deemed unnecessary, unimportant, or inappropriate for the moment, inconsistent with logical thinking, or trivial to meaningful worship (whatever the definition). For example, the person given to intellectualizing worship often talks of the grandeur of the Almighty without ever practicing the grace, submission, faith, and surrender so much a part of communicating with the Holy One.

Such was the case with the woman in John 4. When Jesus started talking about her sin, she quickly changed the subject, intellectualized the process of worship, and spoke about the meeting place. Jesus wasn't at all interested in the place of worship. He was and is intensely interested in the person of worship. He told her the Father seeks those who worship him in spirit and in truth (v. 24). Her initial response was purely intellectual. Intellectualism kept her from worshiping. It wasn't until Jesus revealed himself to the woman and she saw him as the Messiah that she placed aside her intellect, cultural bias, and traditions and gave preference to faith. Intellectual worship is dangerous because it provides little opportunity to experience the wonder of worship. We lack faith when we intellectualize our relationship with and love for God.

Idealism

The second ism in our list of hindrances to worship is *idealism*. This type of hindrance is usually based on the suppositions that worship is only genuine when it includes that which is familiar to our own cultural experience and is only right when it is based on a right formula. A person committed to idealism bases his or her worship almost completely on cultural acceptance, personal experience, and tradition. While intellectualism allows for little or no expression of experience, this approach is based almost entirely on experience. It is at work when planning and commitment to tradition, aesthetics, or personal experience are equated with successful worship of Jehovah. The danger of setting a predetermined pattern or ideal for "true" worship is that the Holy Spirit is often programmed right out of the service. Jesus condemned the Pharisees because their commitment was to outward form. He went so far as to call them vipers (Matt. 23:33) and whitened sepulchres (Matt. 23:27). The idealist often preempts the Holy Spirit's leadership by commitment to plan and structure.

Recently, I read a magazine article in which the author evaluated the worship service of a well-known denominational gathering. In the article, he reacted to the band playing contemporary worship and praise songs for the prelude. "I did not know a single song played during the prelude," he reported, "and I found their aggressive beat and use of drums offensive." He concluded the article by lamenting the fact that there was a distinct "lack of soul-stirring music with warmth and conviction." This brother said nothing about his desire to worship, the biblical mandate to offer praise to God, the flow of the service, the singing of praise, the proclamation of Scripture, or the need to be all-inclusive in corporate worship. He equated worship with his own recognition of familiar hymns and gospel songs.

Idealism is also at work in the hearts of those who see the use of contemporary forms as the true test of worship. Again, successful worship is linked to a previously perceived ideal for programming and not the working or presence of the Holy Spirit.

I recently watched a pastor friend chide his sound engineer and minister of worship because he thought they chose inappropriate CDs for the prelude music. The pastor felt the selection of hymns and gospel songs was too conservative and boring. He instructed the sound engineer to turn the volume up and play up-tempo CDs recorded by well-known contemporary Christian artists. He explained that "the music before worship should be lively and energetic so that young families can visit and enjoy their time together." This brother was more concerned that the church provide a nonthreatening atmosphere for young families than for people to enter into worship with seriousness, reverence, or awe. He equated a perception for ideal worship with his own agenda.

Idealism is a doubled-edged sword: On one side, the commitment is to tradition for the sake of tradition. On the other, the commitment is to being contemporary for the sake of being relevant. In both cases, the motive is unscriptural and methodology becomes the driving force, not the Holy Spirit's prompting.

Imperialism

The third hindrance to worship is *imperialism,* the practice of dominating the affairs of worship by controlling the planning and presentation of a service. This is when a person says, "My way of worship is really the best way to worship. Since I'm in charge, we're doing it the way I want." The prevailing attitude of someone practicing imperialism is that worship is not genuine if he or she is not in charge.

Groups representative of every cultural and theological persuasion within the body of Christ struggle to regulate those having a bend toward imperialism. The sin of imperialism has the potential to influence every fellowship within the body of Christ. Listed below is a sampling of how the dynamics of corporate worship are influenced by imperialism:

The *Catholic* could be influenced by imperialism when rejecting the biblical principle of "the priesthood of believers"—in preference to exclusive leadership in corporate worship by the clergy.

The *evangelical fundamentalist* might illustrate a propensity toward imperialism by controlling music selection for worship—for the purpose of protecting the congregation from unnecessary form and structure.

The *dispensationalist* is influenced by a spirit of imperialism when refusing to allow his congregation to use new and exciting expressions for worship—by denying the biblical basis that God can move in fresh, dynamic, and powerful ways during this age.

The *Reformed theologian* might practice imperialism by making the claim that God deserves only hymns of greatest grandeur—hymns that have passed the test of time—while rejecting anything created for worship in this century.

The *charismatic*, on the other hand, might be guilty of imperialism when making the test for successful worship a new word from God—during each week's corporate worship time.

The *worshiper committed to liturgy* practices imperialism when believing that successful worship is manipulated by controlling the five senses.

The *traditionalist committed to evangelistic soul-winning* is practicing imperialism when asserting that a high energy, enthusiastic, motivational type atmosphere for a service is the criteria for successful corporate worship.

The *believer committed to seeker-sensitive worship evangelism* is guilty of imperialism when the presentation of relevant communication and marketing idioms in corporate worship is believed to be the only effective way to reach an unchurched culture for the kingdom of God.

Imperialism often compels those in charge to design emotionally satisfying stimuli (or aesthetic nuances) as a means for people to know and communicate with God. Imperialism is dangerous because those in charge control all the circumstances surrounding worship—the emotions of a moment, the atmosphere, the lighting, the sound, and so on. Again, the Holy Spirit and his power are overlooked as the motivator and source for worship. Imperialism is driven by the need to control and often for the purpose of promoting a hidden agenda rather than by a desire to engage God's people in genuine worship. On the practical side, imperialism always leads to micromanaging and manipulating the worship environment and the people involved in corporate worship—no matter the tradition, whether evangelical, charismatic, or liturgical. God wants honest, sincere worship, not hidden agendas. He wants the Holy Spirit to be the guiding force in corporate worship, not our traditions.

Isolationism

The fourth hindrance to worship is *isolationism.* This is no doubt the most difficult ism to conquer because it is usually birthed and sustained by fear—fear of the unknown, fear of losing control, fear of displaying too much emotion, fear of showing too little emotion, fear of being unscriptural, fear of man.

The prophet Elijah lived a life solely committed to Jehovah. As one of the most famous and dramatic of Israel's prophets, he walked and ministered in the power of God, predicting the beginning and end of a three-year drought. He stood resolute against the evil King Ahab and Queen Jezebel, predicting their slaughter and unexpected death. (Instead of worshiping the true God, Ahab and his wife, Jezebel, worshiped Baal, the most popular Canaanite god.) Elijah preached against their sin and idolatry, challenging the authenticity of the Canaanite god. In 1 Kings 18, Elijah challenges 850 pagan prophets at Mount Carmel to battle the living, true God, Jehovah. Elijah calls on the name of the Lord to send rain in a time of drought and fire to consume altars erected to the gods of Baal. In what must have been the single most defining moment of Elijah's life, the prophet said,

> O LORD, God of Abraham, Isaac and Israel, let it be known today that you are God in Israel and that I am your servant and have done all these things at your command. Answer me, O LORD, answer me, so these people will know that you, O LORD, are God, and that you are turning their hearts back again.
>
> verses 36–37

God is faithful and gives Elijah absolute and unquestionable victory. The fire of God falls and burns up the sacrifice, the wood, the stones, and the soil. It even licks up the water in the trenches (1 Kings 18:38). All the prophets of Baal are slaughtered. God defeats the enemies of Israel and shows himself as the true, almighty Lord of Lords.

If anyone understood the power of a sovereign Lord, it was Elijah. If anyone knew firsthand the wondrous acts of the God of Israel, it was Elijah. If anyone knew the sufficiency of God's grace in a time of need, it was Elijah. Yet, in 1 Kings 19:3, three verses after the greatest victory of his life, we find Elijah afraid and running—afraid that Queen Jezebel is going to kill him. He flees to Beersheba, then to the desert, and finally to Mount Horeb. There he isolates himself from other believers and throws a pity party. He feels sorry for himself. He feels alone. He is afraid. He tells God as much. He is convinced that he alone in all of Israel worships the Lord God Almighty. God speaks to Elijah and reminds him that others have remained faithful during the nation's wickedness. God did not forget that Obadiah faithfully hid one hundred prophets still true to the Lord (1 Kings 19:1–18). God reminds Elijah that more than seven thousand others are standing true in their worship of Jehovah. Elijah's isolationism led him to depression and a misguided perception of the true work of God.

Many of us approach corporate worship as if we are the only ones "doing it right." We forget that worship begins in the heart. Like Elijah of old, we throw a pity party and convince ourselves (and others around us) that we are the only ones worshiping with a genuine spirit and sincere heart. We use various excuses to isolate ourselves from those who threaten us. We close our ears, hearts, and minds to those who do things differently from what we've grown accustomed to doing within the walls of our own small world. We quickly become isolated. We are soon depressed and defeated. We give in to unscriptural and unholy attitudes toward others in the body of Christ. As a result, the Holy Spirit withdraws his blessings from our lives and we are left to minister in a dry, unfulfilling vacuum. Isolationism leaves a pastor, worship leader, teacher, musician, and church member uninformed, alone, and desperate. Those committed to isolationism make the fatal mistake of falling victim to self-centeredness; the end result is a crushed spirit and a life void of living faith or worship.

Institutionalism

Institutionalism is the fifth hindrance to worship. This concept of worship is based on the view, "We must be right because this is the way *we've* always done it." In practice, institutionalism is hostile toward anyone seeking to create an environment for change. Instead, commitment to tradition is the catalyst for authentic worship. Issues such as relevance to changing culture, sincerity of heart, love for God, and the dynamic work of the Holy Spirit do not play important roles in worship, according to those committed to institutionalism. Rather, worship serves as an agent for continuing and preserving practices and traditions of previous generations.

One of my favorite Broadway musicals is *Fiddler on the Roof,* the story of a Jewish family's commitment to community, their survival during the days prior to the Russian Revolution, and the breakup of norms and traditions unique to their heritage. The family patriarch's undying commitment to tradition is seen in his tenacious love for heritage and unique ability to control the wishes of those around him. One of the defining moments of the musical comes when the old patriarch sings an emotionally compelling song that puts all of life into perspective: "Sunrise, Sunset." He laments the passing of time and the brevity of life. He sees that his little girl has grown into a woman who is now preparing to leave home forever. He is growing old, and the things most precious to his heart are quickly slipping from his grasp.

Some of us approach worship like the old patriarch of *Fiddler on the Roof.* We are much more committed to the principle of preserving the past than of finding practical ways to engage our congregations in worship. We talk in terms of our evangelical tradition, Lutheran tradition, Baptist tradition, charismatic tradition, liturgical tradition, fundamentalist tradition, Methodist tradition, and so on. The Holy Spirit's prompting to sing new songs unto the Lord is replaced by a commitment to the past and a love for heritage. We sometimes stand as guardians and defenders of our own history (what we already know and experience) at the sacrifice of genuine worship. We act as if there is something divine about our traditions, ignore the scriptural admonition to "let the peace of Christ rule" our hearts with thanksgiving, and allow the poisonous venom of a critical spirit and cynicism to destroy our effectiveness in the body of Christ.

Improperism

Improperism is the sixth hindrance to worship. Something is improper when it is not consistent with truth, fact, or rule. It is deemed incorrect or in error. Worship is improper when it is unbiblical, when attitudes about worship are unscriptural, or when we substitute non-worship activities for worship during our corporate gatherings.

About ten years ago I had the opportunity to enjoy lunch with a producer friend in Nashville. Almost every time we get together the conversation turns to issues of worship. During one particularly stimulating discussion, I made the statement that all we do during the Sunday service is in reality worship to God. I continued to explain that to the Christian everything in life is sacred. Since all of a Christian's life should be given as a sacrifice of praise to God, then it is only logical that the announcements, welcome, and sharing of prayer requests in the church service be considered acts of praise and worship. My friend's response was swift and to the point.

"No way," he said. "All of those things can be done and not one moment of worship take place."

I continued to argue, "Not if my heart is right."

"Corporate worship," he continued, "involves the offering of praise *to* God. Where is the worship in songs of testimony, songs of deliverance, clapping and shaking hands with visitors, songs of invitation, giving of announcements, fellowshiping with others, and sharing of prayer requests?"

I sat silent.

"All these things are important to the success of a church service, but they are not worship."

We talked at length about preserving the service times for worship. Much to my own surprise and personal disappointment, I had to confess that my friend was absolutely right. I was guilty of an improper concept of the true meaning of worship. Like many in strategic positions of leadership, I had allowed the most important moments of my public time with God to be crowded out by other things. Perhaps we set aside valuable worship time for a fund-raising promotion. Or we shortchange our most precious moments with the King of Kings to share a video about some community need. I'm sure the community need is important and needs to be communicated, but not during the worship time. We justify our actions by claiming that people captured by the spirit of instant news, drive-thru restaurants, cable television, and the Internet will allow us only a certain amount of their time. Improperism creeps in ever so slightly until finally we begin to equate non-worship activities with genuine worship of Jehovah.

I feel certain that every congregation in every generation has at one time or another faced the hindrance of improperism. I'm also sure we will be dealing with the destructive and vicious results of this hindrance fifty years from now, which is all the more reason to guard with all diligence the time allotted in our services for worship of Jehovah God.

Illusionism

The final word used to describe hindrances to worship is *illusionism*. An illusion is a false idea. Illusionism is the practice of giving an unreal, deceptive, or misleading appearance or a false perception or interpretation of what one sees. In worship, illusionism may involve mistakenly identifying successes in one area of ministry as being synonymous with worship. For example, one may suffer from illusionism when a dynamic commitment to evangelism is equated with successful worship. I am firmly committed to evangelism (see chapter 9), but a church may be actively involved in dynamic evangelistic efforts and never experience genuine worship of Jehovah. Evangelism is not necessarily worship. Now, a congregation actively participating in genuine worship will evangelize, but worship is not necessarily taking place just because people are being saved. The second and third chapters of Revelation provide a set of short epistles to seven churches in Asia Minor. The first church, Ephesus (Rev. 2:1–7), is commended for its zeal, good deeds, toil, perseverance, and ability to endure in times of persecution. Nonetheless, the members are condemned because they have forsaken their first love. They are busy *doing* for God but are void of love, worship, and adoration *for* the Lord of Lords. It is an illusion when we equate busyness, zeal, and commitment with worship of God.

When a local church participates in a fervent and aggressive prayer ministry, it doesn't necessarily mean worship is taking place either. In fact, I am sure there are times when our prayers are so self-centered and so filled with selfish requests that we quickly skim past token statements of adoration or worship and move to a gotta-have list. At best, our worship of God is clouded by the demands we place on the Holy One to give and give again.

A great danger of illusionism is seen when a congregation, pastor, or worship leader holds the false assumption that worship and sin can coexist. The Holy Spirit's sweet, gentle promptings are crowded out by the loud roar of disobedience whenever the body of Christ tolerates sin on any level. Genuine worship of Jehovah will not take place when sin is hidden. It won't take place in a congregation when church leaders tolerate open sin. Sin that hinders genuine worship may take the form of an ungodly spirit toward a brother in Christ, selfishness, gossip, self-centeredness, anger, malice, immorality, idolatry, or any number of actions and attitudes that prevent fellowship with God's people. Colossians 3 tells us to rid ourselves of such things: "anger, rage, malice, slander, and filthy language" (v. 8). Why? Because men and women who harbor sin cannot worship in spirit and in truth. Like the angel's message to the Church of Thyatira (Rev. 2:18–29), the Holy Spirit is against those in leadership positions who go through the motions of worship in service and deed but tolerate sin.

Another form of illusionism may be seen in the belief that worship will take place because specific formulas for service planning and organization are observed. What may work for a worship ministry in Chicago may not work in Kingsport, Tennessee. What may be appropriate to the worship language of a congregation in Dothan, Alabama, or Ivory Coast, West Africa, may not communicate to the people of Indianapolis, Indiana, or Havana, Cuba. The use of specific songs or dynamic Scripture readings do not ensure worship. Only the Holy Spirit can prompt the heart to sing out of love for God and with a heart to worship.

In the fall of 1992, I received an invitation from the minister of music at a rather large church to serve as guest speaker for their annual choir appreciation banquet. I was asked to share with the choir biblical concepts of worship and rehearse several numbers for presentation during the Sunday morning service. I accepted the invitation and in January of 1993 made the journey to the church.

After arriving at the airport and visiting with the minister of music, I began to realize that this congregation was not at all what I had imagined. I thought it was an aggressively contemporary fellowship with a large and comprehensive music program, thoroughly committed to engaging the body in weekly experiences of worship and praise. What I discovered was that it was a large conservative congregation with limited understanding of, tolerance for, and experience with the new worship and praise choruses. Almost everything I had prepared was based on the use of praise choruses coupled with Scripture readings and prayer. I sat and listened with great interest as the minister of music told of his pastor's dislike of and resistance to the use of contemporary Christian music. I remember walking into my motel room, falling on my knees, and asking God to give me wisdom to meet the worship needs of that precious congregation.

The time came for the banquet. I spoke from Colossians 3 on the recipe for God's music—the ingredients for a biblically based music ministry. I sang with piano accompaniment instead of sound tracks, and all in all the evening was uneventful. The next morning came and I presented two sessions on biblical worship. I used familiar hymns and gospel songs instead of praise choruses. The choice of Scripture readings and emphasis on prayer remained the same. I was pleasantly surprised to see the pastor in attendance. The response was overwhelmingly positive.

The choir rehearsals went well. The minister of music and I reviewed the Sunday morning program: prelude, one hymn, prayer, choir selection, offering, solo, and message. "We follow the same order practically every week," he said. I wasn't impressed. I left our meeting feeling rather depressed and heavy of heart. I was certain God was not about to visit us in the rather dull, limited confines of a congregation committed more to preserving legalistic traditions than worship of Jehovah.

The morning came. I attended Sunday school, met with the choir a few minutes before the service, and greeted the pastor with a warm handshake. It was when the service began that something strange and unique happened. The minister of music announced that the congregation was to sing the old Wesleyan hymn "And Can It Be That I Should Gain?" At that announcement several men and women spoke a loud and resonant "Amen," "Praise God." We sang. More than fifteen hundred people joined in unity in singing praise to God with fervor and conviction:

> Amazing love,
> How can it be?
> That Thou my God
> Shouldst die for me.

The singing was electrifying, and the congregation was enraptured with the message of that wonderful Wesleyan text.

Following a brief introduction, I walked to the platform and led the choir in the Dottie Rambo song "Behold the Lamb." The arrangement is a wonderfully crafted rendering by Don Marsh. No sound tracks. No orchestra. Just piano and organ. More than one hundred voices joined in singing the explosive and powerful ending. I held the last note for as long as I could. Then I stood, expecting the congregation to erupt in thunderous applause. Silence. I turned to look, and to my amazement, the congregation was standing. People were weeping. Many had their hands raised to heaven. One by one, people began praising God, shouting "Amen." We stood for several minutes in uninterrupted praise to God. Though the reaction and atmosphere were not what I had expected in a praise service, God came and visited. We worshiped.

I walked to the pew and sat down. The pastor motioned for me to come over to him; he wanted to talk with me. I obeyed, not knowing what he wanted. After a few moments regaining his composure, he put his arm around me and asked if I would preach. I remember thinking to myself, *Preach? I don't have anything to say.* But after a moment or two spent scrounging through my briefcase for an appropriate sermon on worship, I agreed. In introducing me to the congregation, the elderly pastor said something like this: "Brothers and sisters, God has come and visited us today. I've just now asked this brother to come and preach for us. To my knowledge, he has not prepared in advance to address this congregation. In more than seventeen years of pastoring this church, I have never asked anyone at the last minute to come to this pulpit and preach. And I have never asked a musician to stand here and preach the Word of God. But I believe you need to hear him. I've listened with great interest as this brother proclaimed the message of worship to our people. My heart is pricked by the Holy Spirit, and I believe God wants you to hear what this man has to say."

With that, I walked to the pulpit and began sharing the wonder and glory of worship. At the end of the message I sang a very simple solo on the wonder of God's love. Even before I began singing, people began making their way to the front of the sanctuary. Many wept. Hundreds fell on their faces before God. At the conclusion of the solo, the pastor stood in front of those who had come to the front and asked God to give them a heart for worship. We worshiped.

You see, I was the one guilty of illusionism. I was certain that I had to use my new and exciting praise choruses in order for worship to happen. I was wrong. I was convinced that God would not be pleased by sacrifices of praise if they were not accompanied by glorious sound tracks with huge endings and loud orchestrations. I was wrong. I was persuaded that the true gauge for worship was seen in the thunderous applause of a congregation. I was wrong. What I learned was that worship of God happens when people focus with hearts of love and adoration on the wonder and person of the Almighty.

God Can Overcome Human Hindrances

This chapter on hindered worship has been most difficult for me to articulate. Perhaps it is because I am keenly aware of my own tendencies to fall into the traps and snares associated with each ism. Maybe it is because I keep trying to find a nifty list of twenty do's and don'ts as a cure for hindered worship.

I have concluded from this study that although the external hindrances to worship may interrupt the flow and momentum of a service, the Holy Spirit is not hindered by our failed plans. I am sure that extrinsic influences, awkward circumstances, unprepared services, unnecessary moving about during the preaching, child care issues, and sound system problems make for a haphazard, unenjoyable worship experience. But God is not hindered by our small problems. He is not impressed by our elaborate and well-crafted plans for worship. He is more interested in issues of the heart. He is more interested in seeing us cultivate a warm and growing relationship with him, one that is characterized by respect, reverence, and rejoicing. Worship is a personal act that begins with a pure heart attitude, stimulates us in the way we live, and motivates us when we gather at church to relate to God with confidence, admiration, fascination, and adoration. Quoting A. W. Tozer, "Worship is not something stuck on or added, like listening to a concert or admiring flowers. It is something that is built into human nature. Worship is a moral imperative."

The Dynamics of Old and New Testament Worship

> Now the dwelling of God is with men, and he will live with them.
>
> Revelation 21:3

All the world celebrated with great diversity as the year 2000 marched onto the pages of history. Television and network programming highlighted festivities in various cultures and countries. A choir sang Handel's "Hallelujah Chorus" as the clock struck midnight in Toga. New Zealand celebrated with a ritual performed by tribal dancers. Aborigine natives danced to their gods in Australia. A historical ritual commemorating the doctrine of reincarnation was televised from Thailand. China commemorated the discovery of a prehistory fossilized man and the use of fire. Japan merged Buddhist culture and twenty-first-century hedonism. The Czech Republic rejoiced in their freedom from communism by drinking homemade beer. Moscow announced a new Russian president. Poland celebrated with a combination of twentieth-century rock and folk music. An impressive performance of Beethoven's "Ode to Joy" by a full symphony and a one-thousand-voice choir took place in Germany. Pope John Paul II delivered a speech of hope and peace from the Vatican. Jews, Christians, and Muslims met in Bethlehem to watch the release of two thousand white doves. Protestant and Catholic children of Northern Ireland sang folk songs together. Brazilians made music to petition the sea god for success in the new year. The United States celebrated their own diversity of cultures while partying and reveling in the successes of the stock market.

My heart ached as I watched the events of the new year unfold. Amid the revelry, laughter, and excitement about the future was emptiness in people's eyes and loneliness in their voices. No matter the level of celebration, partying, and hype, common to every culture and people are needs of the heart.

The two common elements among all peoples of the world are a need and a desire to worship. And when people do not seek fulfillment of their worship in Jesus Christ, they look to possessions, government, education, systems of religion, and other people—only to be disappointed in people, depressed with government, and disillusioned at systems of religion.

Spiritual, intellectual, and emotional needs are met by worshiping God. God revealed himself and his plan for worship through his written Word, the Bible. The Bible chronicles God's plan to bring humanity to himself so that together they may enjoy a dynamic relationship through communication, obedience, service, ministry, humility, and prayer. When he provided the Old and New Testaments, he revealed his plan for redemption and in the process provided a snapshot of how we will worship in eternity. Let's now turn to an overview of God's plan for worship in the Old and New Testaments.

Old Testament Worship

The Old Testament contains evidence of five periods of worship: (1) early Hebrew worship, (2) Mount Sinai worship, (3) tabernacle worship, (4) temple worship, and (5) synagogue worship.

Early Hebrew Worship

The first evidence of early Hebrew worship begins in Genesis 1:1–2 with the recognition of God as Lord of creation. In Genesis 2, God creates the Garden of Eden, and his presence dwells with Adam and Eve. They enjoy all the benefits of fellowship—communication, companionship, security, and love for each other. God is seen as a Holy God who seeks to dwell with his people (Gen. 12:1–3; Hosea 11:9). When Adam and Eve sin, in Genesis 3, they sever that precious fellowship with God, and communication between the two ceases. They experience death. But God begins the process of creating a new relationship with his people.

The second evidence of early Hebrew worship is seen in Abraham's response to Melchizedek, priest of God Most High and king of Salem. Melchizedek's name means "righteous king." Abraham accepts a blessing from Melchizedek and worships by the giving of tithes (Gen. 14:18–24).

The third evidence of worship and first time the word is used in the Bible is when Abraham prepares to offer his only son, Isaac, as a sacrifice of worship. In Genesis 22:5, Abraham says that he and his son are going to the mountain to worship. God honors Abraham's obedience by sparing Isaac from death. He makes a covenant with Abraham and begins restoring his relationship with all humankind. Abraham receives God's blessing: His seed is multiplied "as the stars in the sky and as the sand on the seashore" (v. 17).

The fourth evidence of worship is when Miriam rejoices in the Lord with song (Exod. 15:20–21). This is the first Old Testament account of the use of instrumental and vocal music in praise. It is also the first record of worship involving passionate movement and participation by both male and female.

Private worship in the early Old Testament times is spontaneous, ecstatic, and passionate. Families participate in sacrifices of praise to God. Public worship is formal and professional. Musical instruments are used for accompanying animal sacrifices to the Lord.

Mount Sinai Worship

Mount Sinai worship is the second period of worship in the Old Testament. Worship during this period focuses on the redemptive acts of God in history (Exod. 20:2–3). During this time God gives the Ten Commandments and approaches his people at the foot of Mount Sinai. The Ten Commandments provide a structure for the Israelites to love the Lord God completely (Deut. 6:4–5), worship him alone (Exod. 20:3–4), and love others as themselves (Lev. 19:18).

Tabernacle Worship

The third period of worship outlined in the Old Testament is tabernacle worship. The Mosaic tabernacle was a tent-like construction, divinely ordained, to provide a place for God and his people to meet. It was portable and symbolized God's living presence among the Hebrews. Here the Hebrew priesthood led the people in worship and gave instruction in covenant obedience to Yahweh. It stood as a life-sized object lesson, vividly portraying the nature and character of God. Through sign, symbol, color, and liturgy the tabernacle served to instruct the Hebrews in God's holiness, transcendence, immanence, wrath and mercy, justice and grace, and covenant love and faithfulness.[1]

Temple Worship

The fourth period of worship outlined in the Old Testament is temple worship. Again, God provides a place where he can dwell in the midst of his people. The building of a permanent site for the worship of God fulfills a covenant God made with his people in Deuteronomy 12:5, 11–26. The temple is the center of Israelite worship. Sacrificial and festival worship, officiated by the Levitical priesthood, stands as a reminder to all people that Jehovah is faithful to his promises. The temple is also seen as a landmark honoring the one who alone hears and answers the prayers of his people.

During the temple worship period, the people develop a genuine appreciation for and use of the arts in worship. Visual arts include engraving, metalworking, woodworking, stonecutting, textiles, and painting. Musical arts include singing, making and playing musical instruments, the writing of songs, dance, and lamentation. Other arts include architecture and design, service in worship, wisdom and knowledge, oration and interpretation of God's law, literature and storytelling, drama and symbolic action, and imagination and creativity.[2]

Worship practices are organized into areas of responsibility during the temple period. King David appoints Levitical priests, skilled musicians, and leaders of worship. A Hebrew choir and an impressive orchestra are assembled, trained, and organized. According to 2 Chronicles 5, a monumental and extravagant display of music in worship takes place at the temple dedication. Trumpets, lyres, cymbals, harps, and a variety of percussion instruments accompany singing. Scripture is spoken with melody and rhythm.

During the temple period, God provides the Israelites with a hymnal, the psalms. Written by King David, Moses, Solomon, Asaph, Sons of Korah, Heman, Jeduthan, Heman, and Ethan, the hymnal is divided into five books or sections totaling 150 songs. The psalms serve an important role in the daily Hebrew worship as they are read, recited, chanted, and sung. Hymns and songs provide opportunity to praise God for His attributes (Ps. 147:1), creative acts (Ps. 19:1), and ruling of the nations (Ps. 2:4). Other songs provide an opportunity for intimate expressions (Ps. 42:1), thanksgiving (Pss. 103, 105), prayers of deliverance (Ps. 142), confession of sin (Ps. 51), and lament and anger (Ps. 45:2–12). Some are used for festive occasions (Ps. 45:2–12), and others are used for processionals (Pss. 24 and 95).

During the temple period, celebration of worship follows the Jewish calendar: Rosh Hashanah (the New Year); Yom Kippur (the Day of Atonement); Sukkoth (Feast of Tabernacles); Hanukkah (the Festival of Lights); Purim (the life and story of Esther); Passover (deliverance from Egypt); and Pentecost.

The religious, political, and social significance of the temple during the postexilic time serves as a catalyst for the New Testament temple and a greater emphasis on worship of the heart.

Temple worship illustrates the importance of God occupying a permanent dwelling place in the presence of his people. The temple becomes a place of prayer, instruction, and divine revelation.

Synagogue Worship

The fifth period of worship is synagogue worship. Although outlined in the Old Testament, its actual development and importance in the life of Hebrew worship do not take place until the intertestament period, approximately 600 B.C. Synagogue worship evolves as the Jewish people are dispersed across the Mediterranean world and the people adapt it as an important center for education and worship.

Emphasis is placed on personal piety, temple ritual, animal sacrifice, prayer, teaching and preaching of Old Testament Scripture, exhortation, fellowship, fasting, and almsgiving. Issues of faith, justice, and mercy, as taught from the Torah, serve as a basis for synagogue teaching. Synagogue worship design follows (in part) the daily Sabbath temple liturgy.[3] Officers are either appointed or elected to positions of leadership in the synagogue. The ministers are paid officers of the synagogue and serve as overseers of the building and its contents, the blowing of the Shofar to announce sacred festivals and the Sabbath, the distribution of the scrolls at times of reading, and the assigning of roles for worship participants. Other officers include elders, interpreters, messengers or delegates, heralds of the Shema, and the almoners.

New Testament Worship

Worship in the New Testament also focuses on God's presence among his people. With the announcement in John 1:14 that "the Word became flesh and made his dwelling among us" came a shift in emphasis from the building, the temple, to the person of Jesus Christ. This time, God chooses to dwell with his people in a new covenant that is purchased by the blood of Jesus Christ. Jesus Christ forms a spiritual temple in the hearts of people through the indwelling work of the Holy Spirit (1 Cor. 3:16–17; 6:19–20). Jesus is the fulfillment of worship.

Whereas God's dwelling place in the Old Testament was the Holy of Holies, God's dwelling place in the New Testament is the hearts of his people. Public and private worship in the New Testament reflect the realization that God's spirit dwells in the hearts of people. Praise takes on a deeply personal dimension of outward and often spontaneous expressions of a relationship with God. New Testament examples of private praise are seen in Mary's rejoicing at the announcement of the birth of Christ (Luke 1:46–55) and Elizabeth's husband blessing the Lord in Luke 1:67–79. Examples of public proclamation of worship include the angels singing "Gloria in excelsis deo" at the birth of Christ (Luke 2). The disciples also sing a hymn before going to the Mount of Olives after the Last Supper in Mark 14.

Worship in the early church serves the role of expressing admiration to God, teaching, and admonishing fellow believers. Psalms, hymns, and spiritual songs serve instructional purposes in public worship and form the basis for singing and making melody to the Lord (Eph. 5:19–20). In 1 Corinthians 14:15, believers are encouraged to sing and pray in the spirit. Emphasis is placed on praising the Lord intellectually and emotionally.

Worship in the New Testament includes preaching, Scripture readings, house meetings, confessions, fellowship, prayer, breaking of bread, singing, and communion (Acts 2:42; 20:7; Col. 3:16; 1 Tim. 2:1–2; 4:11–16; Heb. 13:15; James 5:16). Psalms, Old Testament canticles, and instrumental groups were used in worship by the early church and during the times of the apostles (25 to A.D. 50).

Singing, praising, praying, and adoration to the Lord characterize worship in the Book of Revelation. Worship in heaven includes the singing of saints and angels, music of instruments, shouts of praise, clapping, and outward expressions of love and devotion. Praise in heaven, like that on earth, is a spontaneous response to the nature and character of God. It is the natural response of the heart to applaud and lift up joyous praise when confronted with the majesty and wonder of God. In Revelation 4 and 5, for example, all the host of heaven joins the angels, elders, a heavenly choir, and ten thousand times ten thousand in singing and playing songs to the Lord.

Applying Old and New Testament Worship to the Twenty-first Century

Applications of Old and New Testament worship can be made to twenty-first-century Christians. Expressions of Old Testament worship that may be applied to worshipers of today are: (1) lifting up of hands to symbolize praise, prayer, and meditation (Pss. 28:2; 63:4; 119:48; 134:2); (2) playing of instruments (Ps. 150); (3) bowing in repentance and worship (Pss. 38:6; 138:2); (4) giving of the first fruits as an offering (Prov. 3:9); (5) singing of a new song (Ps. 96:1–2); (6) shouts of joy unto the Lord (Ps. 66:1); (7) reading, learning, teaching, and memorizing God's Word (Ps. 119); and (8) celebrating God with banners (Pss. 20:5; 60:4; Song of Sol. 2:4; Isa. 13:2).

At least nine expressions of New Testament worship apply to worshipers in the twenty-first century: (1) spontaneous expressions of praise, (2) preaching, (3) Scripture readings, (4) singing and making melody, (5) confessions of faith, (6) fellowship, (7) prayer, (8) breaking of bread, and (9) communion.

The countdown to the new century is over. The hunger for worship placed in the innermost parts of Adam and Eve still burns deep in the hearts of people today. God continues to call people to worship, and he calls people to worship as a congregation. He continues to proclaim his Word so that people may believe on him. He reveals and provides a covenant in the person of Jesus Christ and seals this covenant with a blood sacrifice.

God still yearns for a dwelling place with his people. He desires for people of the twenty-first century to know him in his fullness, to seek him with all their hearts, and to develop a deep and personal relationship with him. He is still making provision for people to worship him in spirit and in truth.

One day, maybe during this century, God will make the announcement that time will cease and almighty God will once again be the total focus of worship as people of all tongues, tribes, and nations proclaim in one mighty voice, "Worthy is the Lamb!" Finally, fellowship lost in the Garden of Eden will be restored, and God will be in the midst of his people.

> And I heard a loud voice from the throne saying, "Now the dwelling of God is with men, and he will live with them. They will be his people, and God himself will be with them and be their God. He will wipe every tear from their eyes. There will be no more death or mourning or crying or pain, for the old order of things has passed away. . . . I am the Alpha and the Omega, the Beginning and the End. To him who is thirsty I will give to drink without cost from the spring of the water of life. He who overcomes will inherit all this, and I will be his God and he will be my son."
>
> Revelation 21:3–4, 6–7

The Dynamics of Revival and Worship

> Wilt thou not revive us again: that thy people may rejoice in thee?
>
> Psalm 85:6 KJV

It was late October. Jonathan was walking out of his dorm room, and I inquired as to where he was heading. He responded, "To prayer. Wanna join me?"

Now, what was I gonna say? "No, I don't do prayer"?

I kind of grunted, "Sure. Glad to."

Jonathan led me down the hall to the old storage room, where suitcases and boxes were kept during the school year. There in the left-hand corner he had carved out a space for prayer and Bible reading. An old luggage rack—the kind used in motels—served as a type of altar for prayer. A little table held a study lamp, spiral notebook, and Bible.

A grin swept across Jonathan's face as he inquired, "Well, Vernon, here it is. What do you think?"

"What do you do here?" I responded.

"Pray."

"How often?"

"Every night, Monday through Friday from 9:00 to 10:00."
We got down on our knees, listed our prayer items one
by one, and prayed. He prayed first; I followed. It was
pretty simple and very straightforward, but I was hooked.
A lifelong friendship around the throne of grace began
that night between me and two very important friends,
Jesus and Jonathan Thigpen. As the semester passed, we
met more often, and our time in that little storage room
became more and more important. Our friendship grew
deep and meaningful.

By the time January 1970 rolled around, Jonathan and
I were meeting three to four times a week for prayer—
always at 9:00 P.M., always for an hour. The more we worshiped and expressed love for the Lord, the more God
dealt with us about the spiritual needs of those around us.
The more we met, the more God dealt with us about our
responsibility to share the gospel with our unsaved friends.
This continued until finally one Monday night late in the
month of January 1970, God laid on our hearts the idea
to form a two-man evangelistic team. Jonathan would
preach; I would lead the singing.

During the school year, we traveled on the weekends
to churches, youth camps, youth revivals, and youth conferences. When summer came, we spent eleven weeks in
full-time evangelistic work. Literally hundreds of kids
were saved. We developed a drama and music presentation that concluded with a short sermon and invitation.
Children, teenagers, moms, dads, and in some cases pastors, Sunday school teachers, and deacons responded to
the invitations. We saw adults and young people all across
the country become saved. Some answered the call to
preach, some committed themselves to the mission field,
and others simply gave themselves to God in obedience.
The formula was simple: I sang, Jonathan preached, and
God blessed. Everywhere we went, people were saved. At

the time we had no idea God had his hand on us and was doing something really special through our lives. All through that summer, Jonathan and I kept up our prayer and worship times together.

Those were unusual days in the life of America. The nation was gripped by the controversy of Vietnam, and students were moving from city to city, from coast to coast. It was also an unusual time in Nashville, Tennessee, where Jonathan and I were attending college. Centennial Park is located across the street from Vanderbilt University, and during the late 1960s and early 1970s, thousands of hippies, mostly teenagers, camped out at the park. Many of those young people were transient students taking time away from their studies, traveling from town to town in search of some type of fulfillment in life. Experimentation with drugs and sexual promiscuity was common. The Lord laid it on Jonathan's heart to reach out to the teens at Centennial Park, so in addition to traveling to churches to preach and sing on the weekends, we passed out tracts and witnessed one-on-one to college students at Centennial Park. And young people were saved.

The two of us look back on those years in wonder at how God used us. We didn't know it at the time, but we were part of a great awakening known as the Jesus Movement. God was at work and was moving all across America—in Dallas, Los Angeles, Atlanta, Nashville, Chicago, and Seattle. Revival broke out at Asbury College in Wilmore, Kentucky, and hundreds were saved. Chuck Smith had an incredible influence on the hippies and homeless in the Los Angeles area. What God was doing with us in the southeastern part of the United States, he was doing across the country. We were in the midst of revival.

The body of Christ has experienced revival at various times in history. These times are called great awakenings.

In the Old Testament, God brought revival by moving among his people and showing his great and mighty wonders. Sometimes he brought people to himself through prophets such as Amos, Jeremiah, and Micah. At other times he used the preached word as with Elijah, Ezra, and Jonah. In the New Testament, thousands were saved on the day of Pentecost. Thousands more were saved as the disciples preached Christ across western Asia.

In the first century and throughout the first fifteen hundred years of church history, God used famine, war, hardship, sickness, and government as means of bringing people to himself. God even brought revival when people experienced persecution. The Reformation was spurred on by revival and a renewed interest in the worship of Jehovah. By the early 1700s, God was working in the lives of Europeans as they brought America a spiritual renewal.

Four great awakenings, or extended times of revival, took place in America between 1732 and 1890. Most historians agree that three such awakenings took place during the twentieth century. With every great awakening or revival, whether Old Testament or modern day, came a renewed commitment to worship, conviction of sin, and awareness of God's holiness. When God moves among people and brings revival, people experience an intense desire to know God, show love to God, exalt his name, experience his power, and be obedient to his will.

Historically, changes in music worship styles and open expressions of emotion accompanied every great awakening, and they were characterized by a renewed commitment to personal evangelism, concern for neighbors and friends, passion for world evangelism, and a sense of urgency to tell others about Christ. During times of revival people also recognized the shortness of life, the promise of heaven, and the reality of hell. They placed a renewed emphasis on prayer and had a passion for hearing and preaching the Word.

The First Great Awakening

The First Great Awakening began in 1732 and continued until around 1790. Godlessness, drunkenness, immorality, a severe persecution of Christian leaders, and a violent rejection of Puritanism characterized the end of the seventeenth century. In England, ministers who would not submit to the Act of Uniformity were forced from their pulpits, forbidden to preach, and imprisoned. There was an intense effort by many to rationalize the Bible, the virgin birth, and biblical accounts of miracles. By the end of the 1720s, life in England was morally corrupt.

The Lord used four men to help bring about the first awakening. In England, John Wesley and George Whitefield preached revival and repentance. In America, Jonathan Edwards and Gilbert Tennant preached hell and damnation. From 1739 to 1791, John Wesley traveled more than 250,000 miles, mostly on horseback, preached over 40,000 sermons, and wrote more than 230 books.

George Whitefield was a gifted preacher who had a sincere concern for people, endured persecution, and attracted large crowds. Hundreds followed Whitefield into full-time Christian service, and thousands came to a saving knowledge of Christ through his influence.

Jonathan Edwards was a Calvinist thoroughly committed to evangelism and known for his concern and influence among the young people of Northampton, Massachusetts. His preaching of the sermon "Sinners in the Hands of an Angry God" is often credited as the one single event that began what we now call the First Great Awakening. From 1743 to 1763, between twenty-five thousand and fifty thousand people were converted.

Prior to the awakening, according to one historian, "Music had become a duty, rarely a joy." A host of traveling preachers and singers moved across the colonial countryside presenting a new type of hymn singing that expressed personal experience, joyous times of worship and praise, and long prayer meetings. Strong preaching and an intense focus on music in worship were also trademarks of the awakening.

The Second Great Awakening

The Second Great Awakening is known for miraculous and intensely energetic camp meetings. Around 1790, after America won independence in 1776 and established the Constitution in 1789, many Americans were intrigued with rationalistic literature, including *Age of Reason*, published in prerevolutionary France. Princeton and Yale became centers for skepticism, atheism, and anarchy. Christian students were sneered at, openly ridiculed, snubbed, and excluded from regular campus activities. In some cases, persecution of Christians on college campuses was so severe that many met for prayer and Bible reading in secret.

The Yale Revival. In 1795, Timothy Dwight, a president-preacher thoroughly committed to biblical inspiration, became president of Yale. He preached with passion, relentless logic, and power. At one point over half the student body confessed conversion before the school year's end.

The Camp Meeting Movement, which actually began with the Red River Revival, was part of this great awakening. Two Presbyterian ministers from North Carolina, James McGready and Barton Stone, traveled through the Cumberland Gap regions of Tennessee and Kentucky preaching the gospel. In June 1800, McGready called on the people of south central Kentucky to gather for a four-day observance of communion. Entire families came to the meeting in unprecedented numbers, bringing bedrolls and tents. They spent their days confessing sins, seeking forgiveness for wrongdoings, and repenting from the evils of their pasts.

At the invitation of frontiersman Daniel Boone, Baron Stone preached a series of services at the Cane Ridge Meeting House in Burton County, Kentucky. In May 1801, Stone called for a camp meeting similar to that held in the Red River area. More than twenty thousand people attended the six-day meeting.

Music and worship styles of the Second Great Awakening were primarily based on folk melodies of the Appalachian Mountain regions of the United States. A tremendous proliferation of fresh and innovative music also came through the use of pocket hymnals by Methodist circuit riders.

The Third Great Awakening

One of the most important personalities identified with the Third Great Awakening is Charles Finney. Finney's influence spanned the years 1792 to 1875. Finney was an excellent athlete, skilled marksman, and powerful speaker. He is credited with "inventing" the public invitation, as we know it today, influencing hundreds with his writings, moving and impressive lectures to professing Christians, and sermons on gospel themes.

The Fourth Great Awakening

The Sunday School Revivals of the 1820s to the early 1840s gave way to yet another period of revival called the City Revivals. For ten years leading up to the beginning of revival (1845–1855), America experienced near economic collapse, spiritual famine, and political corruption. Americans were fascinated with the occult, addicted to immorality, bound by commercial and political corruption, controlled by the demons of atheism, and bound by the spirit of greed. The revival first began in Ireland, Scotland, Wales, and England and spread to America. By 1857, a new awakening was well in place, led in America and Canada by Walter and Phoebe Palmer, Jeremiah Lamphier, George Williams, Gawin Kirkham, Dwight L. Moody, Reuben Torrey, and more. Lamphier is particularly significant due to his organization of noontime prayer meetings (beginning in 1857) in New York City that numbered more than ten thousand in less than six months. In Britain, missionaries David Livingstone, A. J. Gordon, Hudson Taylor, and preachers such as William Booth, J. Wilbur Chapman, George Mueller, and F. B. Meyer led the movement. Out of this awakening came the Keswick Meetings of London, Oxford, and Brighton.

Major organizations that affected social change in the cities were also organized, including the United Way, the American Red Cross, the YMCA, the YWCA, City Missions, the Open Air Mission, and the Salvation Army.

By far, the evangelistic team most influential in bringing about change in music and worship during the late nineteenth century was Dwight L. Moody and Ira D. Sankey. This duo traveled across America and Western Europe with the blessings of God on their lives. In 1873, Moody and Sankey began a journey that reaped more than ten thousand converts. Meetings were held in New York, Liverpool, Dundee, Glasgow, Manchester, Sheffield, Birmingham, and London. Estimates reveal that more than two and a half million people heard Moody preach and Sankey sing the gospel.

Ira Sankey, Moody's song leader and ministry companion, was responsible for introducing a new genre of music to the church, the gospel hymn. He is considered by many to be the father of gospel music. Based on popular song forms and melodies of the day, Sankey's songs were composed of simple melodies with a verse and repeated chorus usually sung by a soloist, choir, and/or congregation.

The Fifth Great Awakening

Revivals of the twentieth century may be grouped into three sections: the Fifth Great Awakening (1901–1930), the Sixth Great Awakening (1945–1960), and the Seventh Great Awakening (1968–1990). Due to the advent of new, highly successful, and sophisticated methods of communication, each movement and time of revival was accompanied by the establishment of publishing companies, new methods for proclaiming the gospel, para-church organizations related to the revival ministries, and innovative approaches in worship and music.

The Fifth Great Awakening, which began with a group of students at Nyack Missionary College in New York, soon migrated to the midwestern and western states. As the group moved across the country to Kansas and the Midwest, the members preached, sang, prayed, and proclaimed the need for America to return to Christ and live a life of revival and holiness. In 1905, William J. Seymour, a black, one-eyed, thirty-six-year-old evangelist, joined the Nyack students in a series of services in the middle of the black ghetto of Los Angeles. Meeting in a storefront building on Azusa Street, hundreds of people from a variety of nationalities met for prayer, singing, and preaching. Significant was the integration of believers—black, white, American Indian, Hispanic, and Asian—at the services. The meetings grew into a large and effective movement that spread throughout the southwest and back to the East

Coast. The Azusa Street meetings are credited with the birth of today's modern Pentecostal movement.

Later, during the same decade, Billy Sunday, a former baseball player and athlete, joined with Homer Rodeheaver to hold services across America. Sunday traveled from city to city preaching Christ, forgiveness of sin, the need for repentance, and worship of Christ. Large buildings called tabernacles were constructed for the Sunday revivals. It was not at all unusual for a series of services to continue for as long as a month at a time. Sunday's song leader, Homer Rodeheaver, was a showman and self-proclaimed publisher who organized large and effective choir and orchestra presentations. On one occasion, Rodeheaver assembled more than ten thousand people for a Sunday afternoon choir at Princeton, New Jersey. His influence on the stylistic preference and acceptance of early gospel music in America is still felt today.

Other revivals and awakenings were taking place around the globe during this time. The long and faithful work of the China Inland Mission began seeing fruit with revival in China that spread throughout Asia. Revival of incredible proportions also began with the Welsh Awakening and spread through the British Isles.

The Sixth Great Awakening

The Sixth Great Awakening (1945–1960) came as a result of and in the midst of World War II. Thousands of men and women accepted Christ during the war years, and the evangelical movement experienced unprecedented growth. Immediately following World War II, changes in technology, ecclesiastical influences, and economic, educational, and social expectations altered evangelical culture. Thousands of families moved from rural communities in Tennessee, Kentucky, Alabama, Mississippi, Virginia, and West Virginia to major industrial centers, bringing with them their music, religious preferences, and cultures. John Peterson captured the spirit of that time when he described his experience in returning to post–World War II America:

> I had just come out of the jungles of Burma and landed in Chicago, and here I thought I was in heaven, you know. It was incredible. I couldn't believe it. I'd sit there in the chapel service at Moody [Bible Institute], and I could hardly keep the tears back. I was just caught up in the glory of this, you know. You live in a tent in Burma for a year with no fellowship and you appreciate the joy of sharing your faith. After the war, people had a hunger for God. . . . Spiritual revival was breaking out all across the land. People wanted to know more about God. They wanted to sing about Him and they were busy sharing personal experiences with their friends. One of the things that impressed me was what they were doing with gospel songs. It was an incredible and exciting time.[1]

Evangelists such as Billy Graham, Rex Humbard, Charles Fuller, Jack Wyrtzen, Oral Roberts, Bob Jones, and Oliver Green traveled the country holding revivals and evangelistic campaigns during the 1940s and 1950s. Billy Graham came into national prominence during the Greater Los Angeles Billy Graham Crusades. During that series of meetings, Graham and his team brought together more than seven hundred churches in the Los Angeles area in a corporate, mass evangelistic effort that saw more than 350,000 people come to seventy-two meetings over an eight-week period. More than three thousand professed Christ as Savior. National publicity, all-night prayer meetings, powerful preaching, evangelistic singing, and impressive testimonials from major, popular personalities were all part of the Graham style.

During the decades that followed, Graham became the figurehead of hundreds of national crusades, prayer meetings, intercessions for revival, and a renewed interest in evangelism. Music and worship were directly influenced by the evangelistic efforts, the advent of evangelistic radio programs, secular music, the Bible College movement, mass crusades, and the Youth for Christ Movement.

Musical changes and worship norms were greatly altered during this great awakening. The Youth for Christ, for example, introduced short, easy-to-sing, highly popular gospel choruses to the evangelical culture. These songs were the twentieth-century counterpart to the Sunday school songs made popular during the mid-nineteenth century.

The Seventh Great Awakening

The Seventh Great Awakening (1968–1990) came as a reaction to the sin and devastation of a counterculture known as the hippie movement of the 1960s. The late '60s and early '70s were characterized by materialism, apathy, hedonism, sloth, pride, existentialism, individualism, and independence. The United States was involved in an unpopular and seemingly unwinnable war, and teenagers were traveling across the country in rebellion of traditional values and authority. Immorality, illegal use of drugs, free love, and a sense of restlessness among all cultures were prevalent.

In spite of and into this spiritual vacuum came a broad-based, intense, and heaven-sent revival that influenced the American counterculture, traditional evangelicals, and mainline denominations. Known as the Church Renewal and Jesus Movements, this awakening was, like many of the earlier revivals, led by young people. Thousands of young people on hundreds of college campuses across America professed Christ. Young men and women, once committed to the hippie philosophy and hedonistic lifestyle of the counterculture, trusted Jesus Christ. Revival and the message of Jesus Christ based on repentance, reconciliation, forgiveness, and right living spread from Los Angeles and San Francisco to Seattle, Houston, Chicago, Fort Wayne, Dallas, Nashville, and New York.

Many church historians agree that the Baptists gained the most ground in the awakening of 1740, while Methodist numbers swelled in the camp meetings of the late eighteenth century, traditional evangelicals grew in number during the nineteenth-century awakenings, and Pentecostals benefited from the 1905 awakening. There is little doubt that the kingdom of God was advanced and Christ was honored during the Sixth and Seventh Great Awakenings as nondenominational church groups grew during the large crusades of the 1940s and 1950s and the Jesus Movement/church renewal movements of the 1960s, 1970s, and 1980s.

Jonathan Thigpen and I didn't really understand in 1970 that the movement of God we experienced was really part of the Seventh Great Awakening. We learned, however, that the process of revival is the same for every generation. We learned that true revival begins in the heart of each individual. We learned that revival comes only when we learn and practice genuine worship of God, recognition of sin, repentance, and unquestionable faith in God to do what he says he'll do. You see, revival begins when individuals, families, churches, communities—men and women of all nations—commit themselves to follow the leadership of the Holy Spirit in their lives as the one true source, strength, and supply for worship of God in spirit and truth.

The Dynamics of Biblical Worship

And thou shalt glorify me.
Psalm 50:15 KJV

Imagine this moment. The church service has ended, and I'm standing in front of the sanctuary. As is sometimes the case, two or three people are standing in line to share a word of greeting with me. The first person is a thirty-something-year-old woman. It takes her several moments to regain her composure as she attempts to restrain a visible expression of emotions. She begins telling me how much she appreciated the service and how she believes the Holy Spirit is working in our church. She cannot say enough positive things about how she was blessed by the blending of old and new songs, the emphasis on prayer, and the power found in reading Scripture.

The second person is an elderly gentlemen. He introduces himself and gives me a handwritten note. His only comment is, "I thought you'd find this interesting." He immediately leaves. I put the note in my suit pocket and open it up after getting into my car. It is an obvious and immediate reaction to the service—written on the bottom portion of a bulletin. The note expresses a desire to sing more of the older, more familiar gospel songs and hymns in the worship service. The crumpled paper contains a list of ten or twelve songs. At the conclusion of the list is this statement: "I appreciate your sincerity and obvious commitment to worship. Here are some suggestions that will make it better."

Next in line is a young college-age student who asks some penetrating questions about holiness and what God expects from our lives when we worship. He tells me how much he was blessed by the service. He is followed by a middle-aged couple who tells me they do not like my approach of blending old and new music into one service. Well, I figure I batted .500. While such a stat may get one into the baseball Hall of Fame, the issue here is worship of God not baseball, and stats mean little.

As I step back and look at what is going on in the church around the world, across denominational lines, I see alarming trends that can cripple worship. By and large, there is a serious lack of understanding as to the dynamics of genuine worship (the subject of chapter 2). Issues that are dividing congregations—song selection, orders of worship, clapping of hands, public expressions of praise, choice and style of worship, expository instruction from the pulpit versus evangelistic preaching—are only symptomatic of a greater problem. May I suggest that we are focusing on preferences rather than the true purpose of worship. Consider the following:

> Confusion about the practice of worship prohibits genuine expressions of praise. There is confusion about what is best, good, and right in offering praise to God. There is little or no authoritative preaching that deals with the biblical issues surrounding worship. Music has become the issue, but worship is not about music

alone. There is confusion. Let us be reminded that God is not the author of confusion.

Concern about the shifting of worship traditions and norms is voiced by many in the congregation. Old and young alike express an uneasiness about services because of change. Remember, God has not called us to vain philosophies and traditions. God calls us to worship.

Conflict over the style of music is an issue. Personal preferences of music become the test of genuine worship. God calls us to worship him in spirit and in truth, not in one particular musical style—old or new.

Combativeness in spirit is a defining characteristic of opposing groups. Believers are committed to tradition, historical legacy, and familiarity with songs, which become issues for battle. Again, these are issues of culture and not biblical worship. God's Word instructs us to be gentle, kind, loving, and free of malice (Col. 3:1–15).

Competition emerges between those who prefer the old and those who seek new expressions of praise. Praise and worship is not about competition. It is about consecration and obedience. It is about expressing our love to God. The greatest commandment is to love the Lord with all your heart and your neighbor as yourself.

Psalm 96: Biblical Mandates for Worship

I believe Psalm 96 is one of the most important passages in the Old Testament that may be used to teach us about worship. What follows is a short outline of the five elements for worship found in the thirteen verses of Psalm 96. In this chapter, I use Psalm 96 as a foundation for introducing the essential ingredients for biblical corporate worship. In chapters 7 to 12, I make practical application of the principles articulated here.

The first mandate for worship in Psalm 96 is to *"sing unto the LORD a new song"* (vv. 1–2 KJV). Worship is all about singing to the Lord. We worship by expressing our love, adoration, affection, and wonder of the Almighty to the Almighty. Three important principles about worship are outlined here: (1) We must sing to God. When we sing to God we enter into an arena reserved only for those who have a vital, personal relationship with the Lord of Lords. We share our feelings, emotions, and desires with an audience of one—God himself. When singing to God in corporate worship, we take the attention off ourselves, the personalities leading the worship, and those around us and focus on the one who created us. (2) As we sing, we are commanded to sing a new song. I sometimes chuckle when telling my students and choir members that this passage supports the creative exercise of writing and using contemporary Christian songs. While I certainly do believe there is a wonderful and needed place for new songs in worship, I don't believe that is the point here. Allow me to paraphrase this verse: "Sing every day unto the Lord. Sing expressions of a fresh, exciting relationship with God." The psalmist is referring to our responsibility, response, and reaction to worship of Jehovah. Worship of the Lord should be so sweet, precious, and meaningful that our expression of love for God is evidenced by immediate and spontaneous songs of praise—even a newly composed composition. (3) Our songs of praise are to bless his name. Our songs, private and public, should honor the name of Jehovah. While there is a place for songs of testimony and experience in our corporate services, the clear instruction here is to uplift, praise, extol, and magnify the name that is above all names.

The second mandate for worship is found in verses 3–6. The psalmist instructs us to *"declare his glory among the heathen, his wonders among all people"* (KJV). Worship is all about evangelism. This involves proclaiming to those around us the wonders of God and giving public testimony of what God is doing. We praise God by telling others of his wonders because the Lord is great and to be praised. God is to be feared above all gods. We show him honor when we praise him in public, and there is strength and beauty in his sanctuary when we give him praise.

Worship is all about giving. The third mandate for worship of Jehovah is to *"give unto the LORD"* (vv. 7–8 KJV). All gifts are given as a sacrifice of praise to the Lord. Giving involves four areas when related to corporate worship: (1) Everyone is to be involved in giving. The King James Version of verse 7 says, "O ye kindreds of the people," which implies that every member of every family is to be involved in giving to the Lord. The emphasis is on giving back to God. (2) Glory and strength are the elements of our gifts. The first deals with our motives, the second our energy and work. God doesn't need our money. He already owns the mountains and the rivers, the rocks and the seas, the cattle and the fish. What he wants is our energy and labor, dedication and duty. Just as we sing to the Lord, we give to the Lord our labor. (3) The third element of giving to the Lord involves the glory of his name, which includes honoring the name of Jehovah, giving him first recognition, praising him in public, and giving him the credit for all he does because it is good. (4) Finally, giving includes bringing an offering to the Lord. I find it most interesting that this instruction is twofold: bring an offering and come into his courts. What God wants is for us to come before him in reverence with gifts of substance. He wants us to acknowledge our love for him by giving back to him.

Worship is all about praying, which is the fourth mandate for worship. While not a direct commandment in this passage, it certainly is implied. The emphasis is on *coming before God "in the beauty of holiness"* (v. 9). We communicate with God through prayer. We come into his presence when we pray. Our sacrifices of worship, singing, proclaiming, giving, and more should be couched in sincere, heartfelt, and intense prayer to the King of Kings. Certainly, this involves an attitude of and commitment to holiness. Prayer is how humans express praise to God, and we worship God when we pray. I am persuaded that every time we meet for corporate worship, everything we do, say, sing, and share should be in the spirit of prayer. Corporate worship is perhaps the best opportunity for teaching God's people how to pray in boldness and authority, reverence and love, confidence and faith, and abandonment and submission.

Worship is all about preaching and feeding on the truth of God. The final mandate for worship is also implied. In giving testimony as to how all of creation praises God in verses 10–13, the psalmist makes the statement that God will judge by his truth. The truth of Jehovah God sets us free. *We worship God when we feed on the truth of his Word.* Bible study, prayer, and research of God's Word engage the heart, soul, and mind to worship. It is only natural that our lips and lives praise God when reading and studying God's Word. The Word of God is truth that the Holy Spirit uses to capture our hearts. There is power in the Word of God. In one real sense, the Word is actually Jesus Christ, truth incarnate (John 1:1, 14). We actually meet in the very presence of God when we read, listen to, and explain the Word of God. This is the principle that motivates the apostle Paul in his farewell address to the Christians in Ephesus that they should "take heed therefore unto yourselves, and to all the flock, over which the Holy Ghost hath made you overseers, to feed the church of God, which he hath purchased with his own blood" (Acts 20:28 KJV).

God is praised and we worship as we listen to the Word of God read in public. The Bible gives clear evidence of the importance of reading Scripture in Nehemiah 8. Ezra, the scribe, is instructed to read the law to the children of Israel:

> So on the first day of the seventh month Ezra the priest brought the Law before the assembly, which was made up of men and women and all who were able to understand. He read it aloud from daybreak till noon as he faced the square before the Water Gate in the presence of the men, women and others who could understand. And all the people listened attentively to the Book of the Law.
>
> Ezra the scribe stood on a high wooden platform built for the occasion.... Ezra opened the book. All the people could see him because he was standing above them; and as he opened it, the people all stood up. Ezra praised the LORD, the great God; and all the people lifted their hands and responded, "Amen! Amen!" Then they bowed down and worshiped the LORD with their faces to the ground.
>
> The Levites . . . instructed the people in the Law while the people were standing there. They read from the Book of the Law of God, making it clear and giving the meaning so that the people could understand what was being read. . . .
>
> Ezra the priest and scribe, and the Levites who were instructing the people said to them all, "This day is sacred to the LORD your God. Do not mourn or weep." For all the people had been weeping as they listened to the words of the law. . . .
>
> Nehemiah said, . . . "This day is sacred to our LORD. Do not grieve, for the joy of the LORD is your strength." . . .

Then all the people went away . . . to celebrate
with great joy, because they now understood the
words that had been made known to them.

Nehemiah 8:2–12

God is worshiped when one preaches the whole counsel of God. We give God glory when we apply the written
Word to daily living. Notice the reaction of the people of
Israel in Nehemiah 8. The people listened attentively,
stood in respect, lifted hands in worship, shouted amen,
bowed down in worship, wept, and celebrated. The above
passage illustrates two ways to worship God through the
Word: (1) Ezra read aloud the Word, and (2) the Word
was explained (preached or proclaimed).

The Results of Living Worship

It was 6:30 Monday morning, May 16, 1988. I was
asleep. My wife, Beth, had gotten up early and left for
work. The phone rang. I lumbered across the room and
picked up the phone.

"Hello," I said in a gruff, half-awake voice.

"Vernon?" said the voice of a woman in obvious distress
on the other end. My mother.

"Mom?" I said. "What's going on?"

"Well," she began, "I need to talk to you about your dad."

"Yeah," I answered. "Anything wrong?"

"Huh, well, he's just gone to be with the Lord."

I wasn't sleepy any longer. "What did you say?" I asked.

"Your dad passed away this morning."

"When?" I responded.

"About ten minutes ago," she said.

We spent the next ten minutes talking about the events
leading up to his death. She told me how Dad got out of
bed, dressed, and walked out to a little garden beside the

house. He then turned around, came back inside, sat down on the couch, grabbed his chest, and died. It was that quick. I finished listening to Mom's account of the morning's events, reassured her that I'd get from Oklahoma to North Carolina as fast as possible, and told her I loved her. We hung up. It just didn't seem possible. You see, Mom was diagnosed with lupus nearly twenty-two years prior to Dad's death. Our family always expected Mom to be taken home first. She battled the evils of that disease with grace and seemed to turn every physical challenge into an opportunity to share the gospel.

I bowed my head on the bed and wept. I had never cried so hard in my life. Floods of emotions poured out of my body. After what seemed like hours, I got up, called Beth at work, and told her what was going on. We were able to get reservations on a flight to Durham, North Carolina, and we arrived at Mom and Dad's home in Kinston, North Carolina, late that same afternoon. We visited and shared about Dad and the goodness of the Lord. People from Mom and Dad's church were there. They stayed and ministered to us until nearly ten o'clock in the evening. By that time, my brother had arrived from California, and the events of the day were beginning to take their toll on us.

Around 11:00 P.M., Mom asked if we wanted to have a family altar. By this time, the visitors were gone, and just the three of us (my mom, my brother, and I) were sitting together in the living room. During my growing-up years, our family always began each morning with Bible reading and prayer, usually right after breakfast. Most evenings, right before bed, we ended the day with a time of prayer. The prayer service usually began with sharing of special needs. Then the entire family would kneel beside the sofa and pray. The youngest usually began, and Mom or Dad closed the prayer.

On this evening, the evening of my father's passing, Mom suggested that we close the day with a time of prayer. All three of us got down on our knees in front of the living room sofa to pray—just like when we were boys.

I began. I told God about my dad and all his accomplishments. I told God that Dad was good to us. I thanked God for our life together and for bringing my dad to a saving knowledge of Jesus Christ. I reminded God how much Dad had sacrificed for the cause of the kingdom (as if God didn't already know all this). I guess, looking back on it now, I thought I'd made a pretty good case on behalf of my dad. I didn't pray long at all. I remember thinking to myself, *Who wants to pray at a time like this?*

My brother's prayer was much like mine—simple and to the point. He thanked God for our heritage and the influence Dad had on our family. I specifically remember my brother praying for God to sustain the family with an extra measure of grace in the days to follow.

Mom prayed, "O God, we love you. You are my Lord and King. We worship you tonight."

I remember thinking to myself, *Wow, I don't know if I have ever heard her pray like this.*

She continued, "God, you are so good and great. There is none like you. And Lord, thank you for taking Lee home. And God, I hope he is having a wonderful time with you right now. I hope he is praising you and rejoicing around the throne with the angels. And Lord, I really wish I were there too. I love you so much, Lord."

Then she began praising the Lord for the many miracles he'd performed in the life of our family. It was as if no one else were in that room except Mom and Jehovah. She continued thanking God for his goodness. She reminded God of the many times he'd intervened on their behalf. She reminded him of specific times when their lives were sustained by God's mercy. She thanked God for calling Lee into the ministry. She thanked God for opportunities of service. She recalled by name people who were saved as a result of their ministry and labor. She reminded God of his protection one cold, cold winter night when the car almost careened off an icy cliff. She thanked God for bringing Dad home safely year after year when doing itinerate missionary fund-raising and traveling from church to church. She continued praying for more than thirty minutes. She was captured by the wonder of being with the Lord. I remember saying to God that night, "I don't know what my mother has, Lord, but I want a good dose of it myself." She was at peace in the midst of the deepest, darkest moment of her life. There we were, the three of us, in corporate worship, experiencing the very presence of God. I believe with all my heart that what I witnessed that night was the evidence of a life given to praise and worship of Jehovah. God knew back in March 1943, when my mother surrendered her heart to be faithful and obedient to his will no matter the cost, that she would need a special dose of grace forty-five years later. She began a life of praise and worship as a young Bible college student that continues to be her signature today.

What I witnessed that day in May 1988 was the fruit of someone who had practiced worship all her life. Mom's worship of Jehovah did not begin the day Dad died. Not at all. Her life was a testimony of praise to God. She practiced singing a new song to God, proclaiming his wonders, giving with an unselfish heart, communicating through prayer, and feeding on his Word on a daily basis. That is why she was sustained in such a glorious way during the deepest, darkest time of her life. Mom was a worshiper in private and in public.

God also wants you and me to worship in private and in public. He wants to make us better people. He wants us to worship as we sing new songs to him, proclaim his wonders to unbelievers, give unselfishly of our labor, enter into his presence, and feed on his Word. At the heart of worship is our submission to him in love and obedience. And as we submit and obey, he nurtures. As we worship, he gives grace, victory in time of trouble, and strength during difficult times.

Seven

The Dynamics of Music and Worship (Part 1)

Sing unto the LORD a new song.

Psalm 96:1 KJV

Several years ago I was invited to serve as a clinician at the Hosanna Music Ministry Workshop. The impressively organized and unusually practical music conference is rather prestigious and hosted by the Grace Brethren Church in Westerville, Ohio, just outside Columbus. On one of my first visits to the workshop, I was asked to serve on a panel with four other music leaders from around the country. We sat in a semicircle behind tables on a rather large platform in the front of the building. An impressive crowd of several hundred awaited insightful answers to what were sure to be challenging and stimulating questions. Then came the bombshell, or at least it felt that way to me.

Question: What would you say it takes to have an effective worship and praise ministry? I listened with keen interest as each person responded according to their own life experience. Panelist 1 said, "Well, you've got to have the right band." He explained how their worship and praise ministry is successful because they have assembled some of the best players in the area for the services. The players meet together twice each week to rehearse the service, and on Sunday, everyone is ready to lead worship.

Panelist 2 proceeded to explain that the services in his church were successful because they had the right equipment to facilitate worship. He told all about their use of the latest and most up-to-date keyboards, visual imaging machines, and incredible sound system.

The third panelist, a music educator, gave the typical "educator" answer. He said, "It's all about excellence." He presented a rather effective case that ministers of music should be skilled musicians. "To be successful," he concluded, "musicians must be committed to excellence, well read on the subject of worship, and spend plenty of time in the practice room."

The publisher on the panel said, "Having the right music in your hand is the difference between success and failure for a minister of music."

I sat and listened, amazed at their responses. There were elements of truth in each panelist's answer, but they had overlooked the most important principle of all: Worship is not about music. Music in and of itself is not the criteria for worship worthy of our Lord. Are we so foolish to think that we as ministers of music in the twenty-first century invented worship? Worship is not about the use of favorite hymns or choruses. I'll go so far as to say that worship is not about selecting the ten most popular songs for a Sunday morning service. It is not about purchasing elaborate equipment or erecting impressive audio visual systems for displaying words on a screen. Worship is not about using a praise band, the grand strokes of a timpani, or the majestic sounds of a cathedral organ. And although God wants us to present our best to him, an excellent or poor performance of music in our church service is not a criteria for worship. Our performance may indeed be an indicator of our commitment to sing or make melody unto the Lord and with all our heart, but it is not a criteria for worship. The use of music as a method for proclaiming praise, however, is important as a conduit for communicating worship of God to one another (Col. 3:16). It is a biblical method for communicating praise to God. How, then, should we go about integrating worship and music?

The Integration of Worship and Music

Four principles are critical as we seek to find meaningful ways to integrate worship and music.

1. Worship is not determined by musical style—old or new. Tradition for the sake of tradition will not preserve the blessings of the Lord. Change for the sake of change will not determine future blessings. An emphasis on either extreme will be divisive to the body of Christ.
2. The minister of music and pastor are equally responsible to minister worship to the entire congregation.
3. Acceptance of cultural shifts and appropriate adjustments, no matter the location or age of a congregation, take time.
4. Worship of God is not dependent on the use of modern technology, sound equipment, fancy digital gear, and creative arrangements by wonderful composers. God has given us modern technology and all sorts of gadgets to help facilitate worship, but communication with God has never been nor ever will be dependent on man-made devices.

The disciples on the Emmaus road did not have the latest sound equipment or up-to-date keyboard in hand when their eyes were opened, they saw Jesus, and their hearts "burned within them." The early Christians didn't have overhead projection when bowing in one accord and experiencing the power of God in their lives. The thousands of martyrs who have over the centuries paid the ultimate sacrifice for the worship of Jehovah didn't have excellence in ministry on their mind when marching out before their peers and loved ones to certain death. A genuine encounter with God comes only when we worship the Lord in spirit and in truth. This is especially true when applying the principles of worship to music.

The Bible mandates singing unto the Lord (Ps. 96:1–2)—privately and publicly. There are scores of biblical examples, Old and New Testament, of the use of music in the corporate worship of Jehovah (Pss. 34:3; 145:4; 149:1; Eph. 5:19). Prophets of old sang praise to God in the midst of the congregation, and the disciples used music in their praise gatherings (2 Chron. 5:13; Matt. 26:30). And we will sing with a choir of thousands upon thousands when we gather around the throne and sing, "Worthy is the Lamb, who was slain" (Rev. 5:9–13).

Three steps are involved in effectively using music as an agent for corporate worship:

1. Focus on the purpose of music in worship (Eph. 5:19–20).
2. Follow the biblical pattern for music in worship (Col. 3:1–17; 23–24).
3. Find and develop a creative process for clearly and forthrightly declaring worship (1 Cor. 14:13–18) to God and to one another (Col. 3:16–17).

In this chapter, I will deal with step 1. Steps 2 and 3 will be discussed in chapter 8. Pay careful attention to the illustrations and personal examples shared in these two chapters. Each story is true. Each illustration is shared with the idea that principles are made practical by true-life examples. It is not my intention to use this book as a platform for rebuking, embarrassing, or spotlighting ministries that differ from my own philosophy or practice. In some cases, the names and places of ministry have been changed. In other cases, I refer to the people involved as pastor, brother, deacon, minister of music, brother, or sister.

Focus on the Purpose of Music in Worship

To effectively use music as an agent for corporate praise we must focus on the purpose of music in worship (Eph. 5:19–20). Ultimately, the purpose of music in worship is to sing and make music to the Lord (v. 19). In Ephesians 4 and 5, the apostle Paul, under the inspiration of the Holy Spirit, shares incredible insights on how to integrate music in worship. In chapter 4, he reminds us that we all serve God according to our giftedness. All the works of the ministry are important to God. In Ephesians 5:1–14, instructions for walking in the Spirit are applied to daily behavior. Then in verses 15–20 he uses the metaphor of drinking wine to show how we should be controlled by the Spirit of God. Four principles are applied to music in worship:

1. Walk in wisdom. It takes the wisdom of God to know how to communicate worship to multiple generations, cultures, and ethnic groups.
2. Be filled with the Spirit. Worship and the love for worship only come as one falls deeper in love with God. Paul's admonishment here is for us to be so filled with the Spirit of God that worship becomes

a lifestyle. Just as a person is controlled by strong drink, we are to be controlled by the Spirit of God.

3. Sing and make music to the Lord. He is our audience. Our private and public songs of praise, even our songs of testimony, must always be to the Lord.

4. Give thanks for all things. We should be grateful for each opportunity to sing, share instrumental praise, lead worship, and offer praise to God—in both private and public settings.

Take heed, Satan will always attack and endeavor to hinder God's work when a congregation turns their hearts to singing and making melody, with thanksgiving, to the Lord. There has been and will always be conflict when music and worship focus on praise. When this happens, be careful not to allow music to become the issue. Praise and worship is the Christian's only weapon for which Satan does not have a counterfeit. Satan often robs us of the joy found only in genuine worship of Jehovah by causing us to lose focus of what is really important. The evil one is anxious to capture our motives and ambitions and blur our vision so that we are no longer controlled by the Holy Spirit but by selfishness, envy, anger, greed, and ego. Our love for God and worship of him as sovereign should be the creative power behind our songs. It is when we make musical styles, melody, rhythms, harmonies, performance practices, use of equipment, and even cultural identification the primary gauge for appropriate worship that Satan succeeds in blurring our focus of real worship. We will always find ourselves consumed with controversy if we use music as the test for good or proper worship.

Through the centuries, there has been concern and at times alarm at the use of music in worship. Paul the apostle expressed concern over the use of hymns in worship. Their identity with the unsaved world, and in particular the worship practices of the gnostics, was of great concern to him. Church leaders redesigned worship and outlined appropriate steps for the use of music at the Council of Trent. They felt the music of the church was too fancy and florid for simple worship of Jehovah. Martin Luther was extremely criticized by the clergy because he felt it important to promote and practice the use of congregational singing. The Wesley brothers were criticized for teaching doctrine through music. So intense was the criticism of Fanny Crosby and Ira Sankey's use of popular musical styles in the writing of their music that they were forced to use assumed names when publishing their songs.

Evangelicals associate various styles in music with worship practices. With every generation, every new decade, every new group of leaders in worship have come new sounds, styles, musical nuances, and approaches to worship. And without exception, the style of music appropriate for worship has become an issue.

I remember listening to a well-known gospel evangelist expound on the evils of contemporary Christian music and how the rhythms were of Satan, representative of an ungodly culture, and unacceptable for believers seeking to be obedient, separated from this world, and holy in all things. This dear brother completely missed the point. Satan succeeded in blurring this brother's vision. The issue is not contemporary or traditional music in the church. The Bible does not give any instructions on how rhythm, harmony, melody, form, and tempo should be used in worship. God is much more interested in us expressing praise to him with sincerity and living consistently than in us getting sidetracked by controversy. He wants us to focus on honoring him in all things. In so doing, our communication of worship, our expression of praise, our testimony of adoration will naturally take on the melodic, rhythmic, formal, and harmonic characteristics that he can use to his kingdom's glory.

Concern about Tradition

When focusing on the purpose of music in worship, it is important to recognize the role of tradition. Anytime we seek to increase a congregation's awareness of worship, a concern about precedent and tradition will always emerge. I love the part in the musical *Fiddler on the Roof* when the entire community stands and sings, "Tradition, tradition, tradition." It is true, our worship and praise is greatly influenced by our spiritual and cultural traditions. But tradition for the sake of tradition will not preserve the blessings from the past.

In recent years I have enjoyed serving as interim minister of music at a number of evangelical churches. In each case, it has been my lot to help the church move to a new and often different approach or style in worship ministry. These churches are large, growing congregations and are committed to multifaceted music ministries.

One of the churches hosted a ministry fair during the days of my tenure, a rather impressive display of more than forty different ministry areas in which people could serve. I volunteered to help in the music ministry booth. Assisting me in the booth was a wonderful woman of retirement age who had been part of the church music ministry for the better part of thirty years. Near the end of a very long day, a gentleman walked up to the music booth and began looking at our literature. I greeted him with a smile and invited him to check out the music ministry. I assured him that we had a place for him and proceeded to describe the many areas in which he might want to serve. He smiled and said, "You don't want me. I can't sing a lick." We laughed, and the woman serving in the booth with me introduced the two of us. I stuck out my hand to make the greeting official at which he replied, "I know you. You're the guy who has messed up our music. I don't like you and I don't like your music."

As we continued to talk and he began to drop his guard, the critical spirit began to disappear. He admitted that he didn't like to sing and that he preferred to watch everyone else do the singing. As he continued to talk, I began realizing that he equated a preference of musical style with worship. His concern for tradition was clouding his view of genuine worship. What he wanted from the music ministry and during the worship time on Sunday morning was a performance. He was looking for a group of people, any group, to sing and play songs of worship that were familiar to his vernacular so that he could assume the role of a listener. I would dare say that this brother did not worship—no matter what the style of music. The issue here was not appropriateness of music, preference of style, or a dislike for the music director but a lack of desire for genuine worship. This brother had never learned that worship is an active, engaging expression of love and devotion to God.

Preservation of Cultural and Musical Heritage

We should focus on the purpose of music in corporate worship because people will always express concern about preserving their musical and cultural heritage. Preserving heritage is not worship. And it is not the reason Christians join together for praise. We cease to worship when we make the preservation of our traditions and heritage the primary motive for singing and making music to God.

I read about a group of clergy who met at a Christian college in the northern part of Michigan to discuss the appropriate use of instruments in worship. Many felt the instruments were loud, distracting, and in general, a hindrance to the work of the kingdom. One brother voiced concern and lack of biblical support for the use of any instrument, other than the organ, in the worship of a majestic and holy

God. Another pastor stood and gave an extended dissertation of the evils in using instruments associated with the barroom. "How could God be pleased with such a carnal instrument in worship as a piano?" he asked. At one point a rather divisive and intense moment erupted. In response, a brother called the group to order and asked for a show of hands of those willing to go back to their churches and discipline any member actively engaged in playing church music with saxophones and trumpets. Another brother, the pastor of a large and well-established congregation, stood and lamented the passing of old hymns and spiritual songs. He expressed concern over the perceived lack of respect by a younger, less spiritual group of pastors. He reminded the congregation of God's gift of heritage.

Others made persuasive arguments for Christian liberty and tolerance. Some told of how God was working in their midst and reminded everyone to be engaged in a spiritual ministry. A compelling speech by an older pastor dealt with changes taking place in America and how the assembly should meet people at their point of greatest need. He concluded his speech by making a plea for unity and oneness in ministry. The group spent considerable time talking about worship and how the body of Christ across the country struggles with the idea of change.

During the course of their meetings to discuss music practices appropriate for worship, people argued. Some stormed out of the meeting with fury, showing obvious hostility and resentment toward those in authority. Harsh, angry words were spoken by many. The meeting on music and worship was characterized by hurt feelings, harsh and angry words, divisive attitudes, and spiritual casualties.

This historic meeting convened in the fall of 1870. For three days at a small Christian college, sincere pastors and influential men argued about worship. Not once in the recorded minutes is there any indication that these men ever engaged in any form of worship. I really wonder how much worship, how much singing to the Lord, and how much offering of praise really took place during those three days. The brothers meeting at that college in Michigan were concerned about the need to preserve hymn singing and their wonderful heritage. May I suggest that heritage for heritage's sake will not ensure the blessings of the past any more than will tradition for tradition's sake? These brothers lost their focus on worship.

Let us not fool ourselves into thinking that the problems outlined above are unique to the evangelical community of the late nineteenth century. Satan has always sought and will always seek to rob believers of praise to God. He has won if he can get Christians to spend valuable praise time arguing about "how to" worship. Why? We're arguing and not worshiping. Satan has won if he can distract us and cause us to lose focus on knowing and praising God, for whatever reason—defending tradition, guarding heritage, or protecting cultural meaning.

In the next chapter, we will deal with two more important principles of music and worship.

The Dynamics of Music and Worship (Part 2)

> Sing unto the LORD, bless his name; shew forth his salvation from day to day.
>
> Psalm 96:2 KJV

In the last chapter, we discussed the biblical mandate for singing unto the Lord (Ps. 96:1–2)—privately and publicly. We are to sing as we worship. We began a discussion that centered around the steps involved in using music as an agent for corporate worship. This chapter contains principles for following the biblical pattern for music in worship (Col. 3:1–17; 23–24) and suggestions for communicating worship principles with clarity and purpose (1 Cor. 14:13–18).

Follow the Biblical Pattern for Music in Worship

The first principle essential for effective use of music in corporate praise is to follow the biblical pattern for music in worship (Col. 3:1–17; 23–24). At the core of a successful, long-term music and worship ministry is the worship pastor's commitment to biblical principles of worship.

The Peace of God

First, our worship and music ministry should reflect the peace of God (Col. 3:15). We should worship with gentleness, always illustrating a peaceful, thankful heart that comes from daily worship with the King of Kings. Recently, I had the opportunity to hear a pastor friend present a powerful and exceptionally well-prepared sermon on worship. Everything he said in his sermon about the worship of Jehovah was biblical. At one point in the sermon, the pastor made preference of style an issue. He said, "Worship is not about the style of music. It is wrong for those who love contemporary music in worship to refuse to sing the hymns. Likewise, it is wrong for those who love the old gospel songs and hymns to resist the challenge of singing new songs."

The next morning during the weekly staff meeting, the pastor mandated the staff to include more praise choruses from the 1980s and 1990s in the service. His rationale was that the musicians and worship leaders could not cater to the whim of the aging population in the church. The mandate was apparently issued in disregard of the well-crafted, well-received service of the day before that met the needs of the broad constituency of his congregation. The pastor was anything but gentle in his declaration. His authoritarian attitude, insistence on immediate change by the music staff, and general demeanor did not exemplify a gratefulness for those who labored in worship or, for that matter, what the Holy Spirit had brought to the service the day before. His unilateral decision, no matter how logical or well intended, left the minister of worship and his staff frustrated and in a state of turmoil. Their generally thankful, gracious spirit for ministry was replaced by hurt feelings, uncertainty about the freedom to minister, and questions about the pastor's level of expectation. The peace of God certainly did not rule in their hearts. The atmosphere in that church and with the music ministry was anything but peaceful.

The Word of God

Second, our worship and music ministry should be regulated by the Word of God (Col. 3:16). The Word of Christ is to dwell, abide, live, and inhabit our hearts. The Word of God is to be in our thoughts and control our motives and manner (more on that later). The fact that the Word of God should dwell in us *richly* implies that we should be extravagantly full of knowledge and understanding of the Word. Scripture should control, permeate, and characterize every aspect of our life.

In the beginning days of my ministry, back in the early 1970s, the Lord led my wife and me to work with a wonderful pastor who was thoroughly committed to reading the Bible at least four hours each day. He did this religiously on Monday through Saturday. (He read the Bible for two hours on Sundays.) Over the years, he established for himself a pattern for Bible reading that guided every aspect of his ministry. We worked together during the 1970s, when the evangelical church was in serious flux and turmoil over the introduction of contemporary Christian music, changes in approaches to ministry, and the establishment of new, exciting venues for worship.

Often during my seven years of service, I had to ask for permission to do something new in the music ministry. The pastor gave me incredible freedom to do what I believed the Holy Spirit wanted for the music and worship ministries of the church. On one or two occasions, however, his response was, "Let me think about it, Vernon. I can't tell you why, but I don't feel peace in my heart about making that kind of change." Often he would call me into his office a day or two later and show me a passage from God's Word that confirmed his decision. I cannot recall a time when he was wrong. His understanding of the Word of God permeated every part of his decision making process. The principle of Psalm 1:1–3 is that believers should be so saturated by the Word that it becomes a consistent guide by day and night. When it does so, it dwells in you *richly*. I believe this is the kind of understanding and obedience to the Word of God, in principle and precept, that is necessary for a successful corporate worship ministry.

The apostle Paul also uses the phrase "with all wisdom" to denote the importance of being levelheaded and sensible in ministry (Col. 3:16). The issue of wisdom in corporate worship is crucial to the long-term success and effectiveness of those in leadership positions. God has provided for us a wealth of wisdom. "If any of you lacks wisdom, he should ask God, who gives generously to all without finding fault, and it will be given to him" (James 1:5).

Satan is looking for a foothold, any opportunity to defeat and hinder corporate worship. He has won a victory if he can get worship leaders to act and react outside the wisdom of God—in the flesh, as a reaction to the moment, to prove a point, or to make a statement. God's provision of wisdom is endless. All we have to do is ask for it. When we ask for wisdom as we plan our services, he gives it. Wisdom is essential for the worship leader to determine what is good or best, right or wrong, appropriate or inappropriate, practical or impractical, wise or unwise for the local ministry.

I once had occasion to observe a young, new pastor of a very large, successful but aging congregation violate this principle as he sought to initiate a series of much needed changes into the fabric of his fellowship. Consider the dynamics of his church: More than 40 percent of the congregation was over the age of forty-five; the previous pastor had served for more than twenty years without serious conflict; the church had an incredible tradition and heritage of choral singing; and the music ministry was known throughout the region for their living Christmas tree presentation, commitment to traditional choral literature, and leadership role in music ministry.

In the first six months of his tenure, he led the people to: (1) begin an aggressive church-wide prayer ministry; (2) begin a new children's worship emphasis; (3) establish new worship meeting times; (4) expand Sunday school hours; (5) hire new pastoral staff; (6) develop a new logo and design for official stationery, newsletters, and church business; (7) establish a new approach to evangelistic outreach; (8) appoint a new vision team for long-term planning; (9) move to new property and adopt a ten-million-dollar building campaign; and (10) initiate a completely new paradigm shift toward contemporary worship for the morning services. Any one of the changes could have created problems. In this case, all the changes went into place without a hitch except for the music and worship. In changing the worship and music emphasis, he replaced the organ with a contemporary praise band; substituted the playing of soft, reflective hymns and gospel songs during the prelude with loud, fast-paced, exciting CDs of contemporary Christian artists; all but refused the use of songs from the hymnal in preference to a steady diet of contemporary praise songs; and unashamedly replaced the annual living Christmas tree presentation (a thirteen-year tradition) with an updated drama and pageant. He caused quite a stir. People's confidence in his ability to lead was shaken. Older church leaders, long known for their support and quiet spirit, stood in protest over the changes in worship. On one or two occasions, Sunday school classes passed out ballots and wrote letters of protest about the music in worship.

Let me hasten to say that a paradigm shift in worship practice is fairly normal with any new pastor and may be eased into the general ebb and flow of a service. Each pastor has the privilege as the senior worship leader to structure the worship services according to his own comfort level. But the wisest and most experienced pastor or worship leader will have problems getting people to accept all that this brother sought to introduce in such a short period of time. Perhaps every change listed above was needed, but the ministry dynamic of the congregation will not accommodate the paradigm shift if he doesn't use the wisdom of God and take time to make the changes. The pastor has not been at the church long enough to communicate genuine love for his congregation. The people do not perceive that his love is deep enough to wait for them to adjust. Consequently, Satan has found a foothold to defeat and hinder corporate worship at this church. He won a victory by getting older saints to act and react outside the wisdom of God. Satan certainly succeeded in getting the congregation and, for that matter, their pastor sidetracked. The indwelling Word of God should have guided this pastor. Instead, he allowed personal desire, based on a market decision, to become his motivation in determining right and wrong, good and bad, appropriate and inappropriate aspects of worship. Once again, the use of and preference for music clouded the greater and more important issue—worship.

The Grace of God

Third, our worship and music ministry should be ruled by the grace of God (Col. 3:16–17). The King James Version reads, "singing with grace in your hearts to the Lord." Singing with grace has everything to do with one's attitude. The NIV uses the word *gratitude*. Just as the Old Testament priest ministered sacrifices of worship to God on behalf of the people, our methods for showing, sharing, and submitting worship to God should be with servant-hearts—surrendered to God and committed to one another. In this passage, the method includes teaching (instructing) and admonishing (inviting) one another. Our worship should take on the idea of ministry by edifying and encouraging all the saints.

While the teaching and admonishing aspects of this passage are important, I want to focus instead on the "one another" emphasis in ministry. God calls people to minister. I believe God, in his sovereignty, leads people to a congregation for the sole purpose of ministering to that particular congregation. Others may join. New faces may in time become familiar. Some may move on. What is important is that those working in the ministry understand the mandate of meeting the needs in that congregation. God often adds to a fellowship and numbers increase. Sometimes change takes place. I've heard people on more than one occasion counter concern about change by saying, "Find some place else if you don't like the changes." How can we minister to one another with such a spirit? Are we really being honest to the people God has called us to when we react with such a narrow-minded view? In most cases, those who ask questions do so out of genuine concern for the body. They may even react because of a lack of good communication on our part.

I read in a book by a well-known church planter/ church growth expert that the best way to minister through worship is to select a market demographic, choose music appealing and appropriate to reaching that clientele (country, rock, pop, etc.), and never vary from the goal of reaching that targeted audience. His philosophy is that music ministry cannot be broad based enough to meet the needs of all members of the congregation. He contends that when people start to complain, the pastor or worship leader should tell them to find another church. Now, that concept may work wonderfully well when starting a church and nurturing a new congregation, but it will not work when leading a congregation that has been successfully meeting the needs of a community for decades.

Paul's practice in Acts 16 contradicts the philosophy of targeting an audience and ignoring those outside a ministry strategy. He ministered to (1) those in ministry partnership (vv. 13–15), (2) the needy on the street (vv. 16–18), (3) the folks in jail (vv. 19–34), and (4) the local body (vv. 39–40). In each case, he practiced ministering to one another—even when circumstances were not always the most comfortable or desirable.

Jesus, in Matthew 28:16–20, made absolutely no distinction between those who believed and worshiped and those who doubted. He sought to meet the needs of them all, doubter and believer.

Pastors and worship leaders face the challenge of ministering to those whom God calls—teaching and admonishing one another. Ministers of music and worship leaders struggle with restlessness in spirit when faced with the idea that they must teach, train, and develop their own talent. They are often guilty of looking at other ministries and saying, "Wow, why can't my ministry be like that?" In so doing, they often forget that those ministries are great because someone has been faithful to stay and practice the principle of ministry to one another. It takes discipline and hard work to stay in one place and focus on teaching, training, and meeting the needs of one group of people.

The Work of God

Fourth, we are refreshed by the work of God when our choice of music facilitates worship (Col. 3:16). The apostle shifts gears here. While previously providing instructions for what we do in ministry and how it should be accomplished, here he gives admonishment as to what music is used.

I find it most curious that the Bible remains silent on the choice of musical style for worship. There is no support or condemnation for the use of rock 'n' roll, rhythm and blues, jazz, progressive rock, black gospel, light rock, classical, country, or any other musical form in worship. The Greek translation of this verse (and the corresponding verses in Ephesians 5:19–21) offers no clear distinction between psalms, hymns, and spiritual songs. I believe, however, and I must confess that this is a personal interpretation of the passage, the use of psalms refers to the singing of Scripture, hymns refer to the practice of singing great doctrines, and spiritual songs give credibility to the sharing of personal testimony in song.

Indeed, we should be singing psalms. John Calvin felt so strongly about the literal interpretation of this passage that he forbade congregational singing from any other source than the 150 psalms of the Old Testament. I am of the persuasion that the intent of this passage is that we should teach and admonish one another through the singing of Scripture. Perhaps the greatest contribution the Scripture singing movement has made on the evangelical church is that millions of people have the opportunity to learn Scripture.

I remember attending a meeting in the fall of 1995 and listening to a group of preachers, Christian educators, and denomination leaders share concerns about musical trends and worship practices in their churches. The discussions were intense and continued for several hours. Finally, after several hotly debated speeches on the need to show tolerance and Christian maturity, a rather frustrated pastor stood and declared, "I'm sick and tired of singing Scripture. I'll be glad when we can get back to singing good ol' fashioned gospel songs about soul-winning and revival," to which arose thunderous "amens" across the building. I thought to myself, "Excuse me, you don't want to sing Scripture?" It really is difficult to build a case against the singing of Scripture. Make no mistake about it, the biblical instruction is clear for us to hide the Word of God in our hearts. Singing Scripture facilitates that process.

Indeed, we should be singing hymns. Praise God for the way our evangelical churches have turned to using choruses in their worship of Jehovah. I believe we can see an increase in congregational singing and participation because of our use of worship and praise choruses. However, in all too many congregations, with the use of these choruses has come an abandonment of hymns. The greatest argument for using older hymns and gospel songs is that through their use we teach doctrine. Pastors and worship leaders who have forsaken the use of hymns in deference to newly composed worship and praise songs forget Paul's admonition to teach and admonish one another. Even though I heartily applaud more congregational participation in worship, I am alarmed at the sheer lack of theological integrity in many of the songs written today. The Wesley brothers wrote more than four thousand hymns specifically designed to teach doctrine and in obedience to the scriptural admonition of Colossians 3:16. The contribution of John and Charles Wesley, William Cowper, Isaac Watts, and more than fifty other hymn writers of the eighteenth century is seen in their persistent and consistent use of melody to teach the doctrines of God. We desperately need songs that do so today.

Indeed, we should be singing spiritual songs. The Greek transliteration of spiritual songs is non-carnal music. Our spiritual songs should provide a clear testimony of what God is doing in our lives. There should be no room for misunderstanding as to the clear presentation of the gospel in our church music.

I am persuaded that carnal here applies to music associated with cultures inconsistent with Christian behavior.

In recent years, I have come to the conclusion that we are sadly mistaken if we believe music is amoral and musical styles or form make little or no difference in a successful worship and praise ministry. Granted, the Bible has nothing to say about rhythms, harmonies, form, and melody, but there is a wealth of instruction on avoiding the appearance of evil. I am certain that our worship and praise music should not imitate the music of the ungodly, carnal world around us, no matter how convincing and theologically profound the text.

I have missionary friends actively involved in ministry to the Lobe tribe in Ivory Coast, West Africa. They are thoroughly committed to helping their new converts develop a hymnody indigenous to the culture and language of the region. In expressing praise to God, however, the native Christians consistently express concern over the use of music associated with songs witch doctors use in calling forth evil spirits. They believe that unsaved natives will misunderstand the praise to Jehovah, the living God, if the music sounds too much like that used by witch doctors. The Holy Spirit taught these African brothers and sisters that spiritual songs refer to non-carnal music.

Non-carnal not only applies to musical form and cultural identification but to the presentation, motive, intent, and performance atmosphere of the musicians. Singing with grace in your heart to the Lord speaks to the issue of motive. Our motive for administrating worship should reflect a heart that sings a song of grace to the Lord.

May I suggest that so much of what we do in the name of Christian worship is in the flesh, driven by a hidden agenda, done for the approval of others, and to show off our abilities. The Bible gives a clear mandate that our manner or deportment, whether in word or deed, should demonstrate a sincere commitment to offer God praise with grateful hearts of worship (Col. 3:17). There is no room for hidden agendas. The apostle writes:

> And whatever you do, whether in word or deed, do it all in the name of the Lord Jesus, giving thanks to God the Father through him. . . . Whatever you do, work at it with all your heart, as working for the Lord, not for men, since you know that you will receive an inheritance from the Lord as a reward.
>
> Colossians 3:17, 23–24

Develop a Process for Communicating Worship

The final principle for effective use of music in corporate praise involves the ability to communicate worship. I deliberately use the phrase "communicate worship" for two reasons: (1) Worship involves an aspect of communicating *to* God: I sing *to* God; I pray *to* God; I express love *to* God; I give all worship *to* God. The Holy Spirit enables us to communicate, as it were, with God. As we worship and honor the living Lord, he communicates to us by giving a sense of peace, purpose, joy, and contentment. (2) The second type of communication involves communicating through song, Scripture, and prayer. The worship leader communicates in such a manner that people will engage in worship. The challenge we face in the twenty-first century is to communicate on cultural, generational, and sometimes educational levels. Remember, we want God's people to engage in worship. To make that happen, we sometimes have to design creative ways to articulate clearly biblical principles, practices, and processes for corporate worship. This involves communicating worship. The apostle Paul writes about the need for good communication in 1 Corinthians 14:15: "What is it then? I will pray with the spirit, and I will pray with the understanding also: I will sing with the spirit, and I will sing with the understanding also" (KJV).

Corporate worship should be designed so that people can readily apply biblical principles to daily life and live with a sense of worship in their hearts all week. This means that worship leaders need to develop good communication skills. It also means that worship leaders must be sensitive to their audience's ability to perceive and understand. Some people call this process a worship language. I'm not referring to a special gift given by the Holy Spirit to a worship leader or worshiper; rather, I'm referring to a process of communicating in a manner that will enable worshipers to understand and participate in the worship ministry— breaking down walls of communication so that everyone in the audience feels free to share in worship. Perhaps the following illustration will explain this principle.

I remember hearing about a group of missionaries who went into a country in West Africa and insisted that all new converts adopt the worship songs of the Western church. So every Sunday these new tribal believers would stand and sing the doxology to the Lord. The missionaries could not understand why their new converts did not sing with heartfelt emotion and passion. It was not until years later, when missionaries began teaching new converts how to use their own musical style, familiar melodies, and rhythms as a method for praising the living God, that the national Christians began singing songs of praise to God. Their point of reference for singing was different from that of their missionary friends. They sang in a modified pentatonic scale, not the traditional diatonic scale familiar to most Western music. Simply put, their cultural experience for singing did not include all the notes in the missionary's melodic scale. So every time they sang the doxology, they naturally and unknowingly modified the tune to fit their own pentatonic scale. It was truly a mess. Likewise, we are exceedingly unwise to push congregations to accept music for worship in a style or of a culture they don't know, live in, experience, or understand.

I believe communication differences are at the heart of our worship and praise controversy. I suggest that pastors, ministers of music, and worship leaders often communicate in languages not clearly understood by the entire congregation. When people's understanding of culture is blurred, they begin to criticize and complain. Our responsibility is to teach people of all ages to clearly see and understand the joy of worship. By so doing, people learn to respect differences of expression in music because it is worship. Older saints become tolerant of the younger; younger Christians respect the heritage and wonder of preceding generations. No longer should I ask, "Which music should I use in worship—contemporary or traditional?" We should focus our attention as worship leaders and pastors on patiently and lovingly learning about our people so that we may effectively communicate and lead worship within the framework of their understanding—their culture. It takes time to carefully move people from where they are—age, culture, and life experience—to a place where they can develop appreciation for all expressions of worship.

Perhaps at the heart of the communication of music and worship is a better understanding of the role worship pastors are to have in the local church. We are engaged in a priestly ministry. The pastor is shepherd of the flock of God. He is set aside for service. He serves as the senior pastor or bishop of the congregation—the chief overseer. As such, he is responsible for assuming the role of senior worship leader. If we use the Old Testament as a model for ministry, the musicians are worship leaders also set aside for ministry. They are, in every sense of the word, priests.

Those serving as worship leaders and ministers of music have the unique responsibility of standing alongside the chief priests (pastors) and providing ministry to the entire congregation.

Ephesians 4 provides a wonderful exposition of the different responsibilities of those called into the ministry. God gives areas of service according to a person's giftedness. Pastors and ministers of worship have the responsibility of meeting the needs of people within the framework of their own life experiences and culture. Our good will be evil if we do anything less.

A few years ago, a pastor friend called and asked if we could visit and discuss his church's need for a minister of music. We met for an extended lunch time and discussed the challenges in his church. He said, "Let me explain a little about the dynamics of our church. On any given Sunday morning we have three congregations gathered in one room: those that only want to sing the hymns and gospel songs of the nineteenth century, the group that is committed to an exclusive use of worship and praise songs, and . . ." he paused, took a deep breath, and continued, "well, then there is the crowd that isn't happy unless they can tap their toe, clap their hands, and cry a little bit while singing their favorite Southern gospel quartet number." He went on, "There are two kinds of reactions when that screen comes down and we start singing choruses: Some show an obvious expression of disdain. Others look as though they are about to be part of the next great awakening. What's a pastor to do? I'll tell you Vernon, the man we hire as our worship pastor must have the ability to communicate and lead worship to all three groups with heartfelt sincerity."

This pastor should be commended. He and his church leaders took the better part of two years to secure a man suitable to the task. While the search committee was busy searching for a new worship leader, the pastor commenced to (1) preach sermons on worship, (2) share his heart for communicating principles of worship from the pulpit, (3) broaden his own musical horizons to include styles not necessarily of his own preference, (4) hold special workshops with an emphasis on the principles of biblical worship, (5) practice worship with all God's people in the morning service, (6) make his desire for the fellowship to become a worshiping congregation an item of constant and persistent public prayer, and (7) wait for God to change hearts. He carefully communicated to all the people God's plan for worship, clearly defined the role of a new worship pastor, and cautiously prepared the people for change. Consequently, when that congregation found a young man willing to come and lead their worship, they found a person uniquely gifted at blending a variety of cultural styles in music and drama into one cohesive offering of praise. This pastor showed mature and wise restraint in waiting to initiate change until the congregation's frame of reference was broadened. He showed genuine love and concern for the people of his congregation by seeking to meet their broad, diverse worship needs.

In summary, God has given us a wonderful mandate for using music in our worship. First, we are to sing to the Lord—publicly and privately (Ps. 96:1–2). Second, we are to follow the biblical pattern for worship (Col. 3:1–17, 23–24). This involves the peace of God, the Word of God, the grace of God (doing worship with an attitude of gratitude), and the work of God. Third, we are to communicate worship in a language that people can quickly identify. This kind of communication involves taking into consideration a worshiper's cultural orientation, generational identity, and educational experience.

One final word about worship and the working of the Holy Spirit needs to be made. We can sing songs, follow all the rules for a biblically based music and worship ministry, and communicate in a language that is clearly understood by all and yet never really engage people in worship. The Holy Spirit is the catalyst for prompting people to worship. The Holy Spirit promises to bless our efforts only as we give ourselves to God with hearts of love, adoration, and commitment to him as Lord. We serve God not men: "Whatever you do, work at it with all your heart, as working for the Lord, not for men, since you know that you will receive an inheritance from the Lord as a reward. It is the Lord Christ you are serving" (Col. 3:23–24).

The Dynamics of Evangelism and Worship

Declare his glory among the nations.

Psalm 96:3

Worship is about evangelism. Evangelism involves proclaiming the wonders of God to the unsaved community around us. Evangelism takes place through worship when out of our love for the Almighty we are motivated to tell others about Christ.

God sent his Son to redeem men and women, boys and girls from the curse of sin so that they could become worshipers. Jesus died to save us from eternal hell, but he also died to redeem us so we can enjoy a dynamic, loving relationship with God. God has passionate love for people. He longs for men and women everywhere to be saved. We are made righteous and adopted as sons of God, and we become joint heirs and receive eternal life all because of salvation by grace through faith. Why? So that we can enjoy God forever.

If our passion and love for God is not the motivating force behind our love for people, then evangelism, and the thrill of seeing people brought to a saving knowledge of Jesus Christ, becomes nothing more than a method for keeping church attendance high and conquering the foe. God calls us, however, to preach the gospel, reach the unreachable, and mend the brokenhearted.

Years ago a controversy of sorts arose, primarily among the more conservative, fundamental denominations, over issues of evangelism and "walking a deeper life." Many preachers taught that a person had to choose between evangelism—which they called "soul-winning"—and worship—which they called "the deeper life." The irony of this issue is that both terms, "soul-winning" and "deeper life," are not even found in the Bible. Those espousing the notion of "soul-winning" took their premise from Proverbs 11:30: "He who wins souls is wise." The "deeper lifers," as they were called, found refuge in Philippians 3:10: "I want to know Christ." Both groups took an element of truth out of context and to an extreme.

Looking back on it, I'm sure the soul-winning/ deeper-life battle was one of those controversies straight from the mind of Satan. Satan does that kind of thing to side-track believers and distract them from what is important.

God wants us to be concerned about the souls of men and women. He wants others to know him, his power, and the fellowship of his sufferings. And God wants our relationship with him to go deeper. There isn't a choice to be made. God wants a balance in our lives. He wants a church, a congregation, to be both a soul-winning haven for the unsaved and a fellowship deeply committed to knowing God in all his fullness.

Worship as We Evangelize

Acts 16 contains the historical account of the travels of Paul the apostle, Silas, Luke, and young Timothy as they moved from town to town preaching and teaching the gospel of Jesus Christ. They are prevented by the Holy Spirit from going first to Asia and later to Bithynia. Finally, again by the leadership of the Holy Spirit, they are permitted to go to Macedonia and on to Philippi.

By the time we get to verse 25, Paul has delivered a young woman from demonism, appeared before the magistrates, and has been charged with ruining a lucrative business. Paul and Silas are taken by guards, beaten, and thrown into prison.

The activity of verses 16–24 serves as the prelude to what must have been an incredible worship service—a corporate worship gathering that resulted in a premier evangelistic opportunity. The Bible records that Paul and Silas used their imprisonment as an opportunity for worship, and what follows in Acts 16:25–34 is a six-step process of worship that leads to evangelism.

First, they met in a place of worship. Granted, this wasn't the most eloquent cathedral, most elaborate sanctuary, most scenic hillside, or quaintest chapel. After all, this was the city jail. And the inner jail at that. But Paul and Silas turned that jail cell into a place of worship. And God was exalted.

Second, they gave priority to worship. It was midnight. Most people are in bed asleep at midnight, even in a prison. These brothers decided it was much more important to spend time praying and singing to God than sleeping. And God was honored by their worship.

Third, the people worshiped together. The prisoners listened as Paul and Silas prayed and sang praises to the Lord. Paul and Silas used this as an opportunity to proclaim the wonders of God. It was soul-winning in action. The unbelievers witnessed the praise of God's people. And God's Spirit of conviction moved in their hearts.

Fourth, they presented praise to God. Their praise was *unto* the Lord. I wonder what they sang? I wonder what they prayed? I wonder how they worshiped together? Imagine the scene: Two devoted followers of Christ, imprisoned for casting a demon out of a young girl, sitting in the inner prison, hands and feet in stocks, singing and praising God!

I'm sure most of us would have grumbled. We certainly would have complained about the heat, air conditioning, or general atmosphere. Not these guys. They simply worshiped Jehovah. And God came and visited them in prison.

The earth shook and immediately all the doors of the prison were opened. Everyone's hands and feet were loosed. Paul and Silas were free to go. But they didn't! They had a greater calling.

Fifth, they preached Christ. When the doors opened, the keeper of the prison drew his sword with all intentions to kill himself. Paul shouted, "Do yourself no harm, for we are all here." Paul and Silas could have fled. Instead, they stayed in the inner jail. I suspect they knew their worship was about to turn into an evangelism conference.

The Bible says that when the keeper of the prison realized what had happened, he trembled and fell at the apostles' feet asking, "What must I do to be saved?" Paul and Silas had the answer. Without hesitating they proclaimed, "Believe in the Lord Jesus, and you will be saved—you and your household" (vv. 30–31). They preached the gospel. And God blessed their commitment to worship.

Sixth, the Holy Spirit produced fruit. They worshiped by proclaiming the wonders of God, the Holy Spirit blessed, and the keeper of the prison and his family believed and rejoiced together. And God was blessed as the family became worshipers.

Somehow, I never cease to be amazed at how God works. He gave Paul and Silas an attitude that had a major effect on their methods for evangelism. Not once during Paul and Silas's incarceration did the issues of deeper life and evangelism come up. They were not concerned about their philosophy of worship measuring up to the practice of those around them. The issue of doing something out of a sense of obligation rather than obedience did not enter into the picture. They were driven by a conscious concern for worship of Jehovah.

Lessons for Today

What lessons should we learn from the corporate worship service in the Philippian prison?

First, the unsaved world watches when we worship (Acts 16:25). Can you imagine how each prisoner must have been captured by the passion and spirit Paul and Silas had for worship? Paul and Silas were confined to the inner jail, which means they were in the middle—a spectacle for all to see—a position of humiliation and embarrassment. Paul and Silas turned that inner prison into a sanctuary for corporate worship. They proclaimed the wonders of God, and the heathen listened.

The second lesson to be learned also involves our public testimony. *People watch how we react much more than how we act (Acts 16:28–31).* Paul and Silas did not allow the circumstances surrounding them to temper their worship of God. Today, we would say, "They were true professionals," or, "They didn't lose their cool." In reality, they were filled with the Spirit of a Holy God. As a result of their calm reaction and sensible action, God was honored.

There is not one indication that Paul and Silas were full of criticism or a spirit of unhappiness. I surmise most of us would have cried out against the unfair, unrighteous, and undeserved treatment dealt to us by ungodly magistrates. Imagine the embarrassment. Paul and Silas had their clothes torn from their bodies and then were beaten with rods—a form of public ridicule and humiliation. I think we would have cried out that the government was using unconstitutional methods of punishment. Not Paul and Silas. They kept a Christ-honoring, sweet spirit. They didn't try to prove a point, set an agenda, set the record straight, stand up for their rights, promote equal rights, push through their concepts for freedom, or develop an organization for political justice. They simply worshiped, and God did the rest.

The third lesson to be learned from their worship service is that *people are much more prone to listen to what we say about the gospel when they sense a genuine concern on our part for their needs.* I have wondered about the prayers Paul and Silas offered while in jail. I am led to think they might have openly prayed for the magistrates and for those in authority over them, including the keeper of the jail. After all, this same Paul wrote, under the inspiration of the Holy Spirit:

> I urge, then, first of all, that requests, prayers, intercession and thanksgiving be made for everyone— for kings and all those in authority, that we may live peaceful and quiet lives in all godliness and holiness. This is good, and pleases God our Savior, who wants all men to be saved and to come to a knowledge of the truth.
>
> 1 Timothy 2:1–4

It seems certain the keeper of the jail was persuaded that Paul and Silas had fled. Instead, Paul and Silas stayed in their places and restrained the jailer from committing suicide (Acts 16:28). So impressed was the jailer that he fell down trembling before Paul and Silas. He didn't ask Paul and Silas about their philosophy of worship, soulwinning, or church growth. They were committed to lifestyle worship, and God honored their faithfulness. The jailer simply asked, "What must I do to be saved?"

The fourth lesson to be learned from this jailhouse experience is that *Satan will always try to hinder evangelistic efforts, most often by masking the truth, distracting us from worship, and diminishing our credibility.* We see Paul's concern about the clear presentation of the gospel in the way he reacted to the young girl (vv. 16–19) who followed them proclaiming, "These men are servants of the Most High God, who are telling you the way to be saved" (v. 17). There was an element of truth in her words, but the demon living in this young girl masked the message and hindered a clear gospel presentation. The very fact that she went with Paul and Silas identified their work with mystics and spiritists, something Paul did not want to happen. So Paul, under the authority of the Holy Spirit and in the name of Jesus Christ, cast the demon out of the young girl. Apparently, she was a slave and her masters were using her mystic powers as a means for making money. Obviously, they became angry.

It's no different in our arena of corporate worship today. A host of would-be worship leaders and profiteers are jumping on the worship and praise bandwagon in the name of Jesus. They talk worship, preach the truth of worship, and act as if they understand biblical worship. Sometimes they boast an all-star praise band, hold worship seminars, flaunt recordings and videos of the incredible workings of God, boast of unforgettable and sensational experiences with the Almighty, and command a throng of followers. But at the end of the day, they mask the truth of the gospel by misguided motives, harm the gospel's effect by their inconsistencies and impure actions, and march over sincere expressions of praise with the measuring stick of commercial success. They do not understand the need for repentance in worship, and few come to a saving knowledge of Christ. Moreover, the freshness found in a broken spirit is rarely evident. Not once did Paul and Silas seek monetary gain from their experience. They were committed to the worship of God and the presentation of the gospel.

Satan thought he'd won the battle when Paul and Silas were thrown into that prison cell. It was the Sabbath, and they would certainly be distracted from their worship of God. Satan always seeks to distract God's people from worship. He knows that a worshiping congregation will be a soul-winning congregation. He knows that he has lost the war when God's people go to their knees in prayer and then arise to enter the streets with the gospel. Paul and Silas fought Satan's attempt to distract their worship by making the jail cell a cathedral of praise.

Satan sought to damage their credibility, and he almost succeeded. Their credibility was undoubtedly questioned as they stood and endured the disgrace of public punishment. But their credibility was restored as they lifted genuine praise to the Lord. I am persuaded that only through praise and worship of Jehovah can misinformation of truth by the evil one be battled. Remember, Satan is the deceiver, the father of all lies, and the master of misrepresentation of truth.

Another lesson to be learned from the jailhouse experience is that *worship-evangelism will always cause a stir—especially when it affects the salaries of those doing wrong (vv. 16–19)*. The men making accusations against Paul and Silas were angry because they had lost an important source of revenue. The unsaved will come to a saving knowledge of Christ when God's people worship in fullness and truth. The pimp doesn't care if his prostitute gets saved—that's a personal matter. But take away the finances brought in by that unfortunate girl and he'll immediately become interested in what's going on. The owner of the local liquor store could care less about the worship of God's people until those same people, transformed by the power of God, stop coming in on Saturday nights to load up on booze.

Ron Owen, in his new book, *Return to Worship*, calls what takes place at conversion "repentant worship." It is out of love for God that a person receives Christ into his or her heart and turns from sin. That kind of worship will cause a serious stir.[1]

My parents were missionaries to Alaska. My mother was particularly gifted at knowing how to share the gospel with hurting people. During one particularly fruitful time of ministry, my mother saw several girls who worked at a prominent night club come to a saving knowledge of Christ. It began with one striptease dancer named Dorothy, who was saved, left the club, and shared the gospel with her friends. Almost immediately after her conversion, she offered to host prayer and praise services in her home, and she asked my mother to lead worship and share a gospel message. One by one, the nude dancers from this night club were saved, and the owner was having problems finding girls to take off their clothes. His business was seriously threatened by the gospel.

Around ten o'clock on one particular Saturday night, I was getting ready for bed. The phone rang and I ran into the living room to retrieve the call. A rough-sounding voice asked if Rev. Whaley was in. I told him my dad was home and that I'd get him.

Dad answered the phone, "Rev. Whaley speaking."

The voice on the other end of the line said, "Rev. Whaley, you're going to die."

There was a click and then a dial tone.

Well, I must say, it certainly got my parents' attention. They called the police and an investigation insued. Years later, we found out that the owner of that night spot had made the call. Satan will always try to hinder our efforts to evangelize.

Another lesson to be learned from Paul and Silas's worship service is that *evangelism is most effective when it is an extension of our own worship—personal and public.* Paul and Silas's efforts did not take place according to market plans, demographic studies, surveys, or strategic planning. Their soul-winning was an outgrowth of their own personal time with God. Their actions were in direct response to the leadership of the Holy Spirit. Philippi was a colony—not a big city. Paul wanted to go to Asia but was prohibited by the Holy Spirit. Again, he wanted to go into Bithynia and Mysia, but the Spirit of God did not permit him to preach. In Philippi, Paul witnessed the conversion of Lydia (and her subsequent call into full-time ministry), the conversion of a young girl, an opportunity to go before the magistrates with the gospel, and the conversion of an entire family. Paul was twice restrained from going to other places because God had better plans. There is absolutely no way of knowing the level of influence the jailer and his family had in that town. I'm sure many more were brought to Christ because of his testimony of grace.

The final lesson to be learned from the jailhouse worship service is that *God is much more concerned about evangelism than we could ever be. He will prepare the way for us.* Our responsibility is to go to those who need to know Christ. God wants us to be ready and willing vessels for his kingdom use. Paul and Silas did not have to manipulate or manhandle the situation; God had already prepared the heart of each listener. He still brings people to an understanding of salvation in the same way. He prepares hearts through the power of the Holy Spirit. Paul responded with a quick and direct answer when the jailer said, "What must I do to be saved." He didn't make apologies, water down the truth of the gospel, or endeavor to explain the how and why of Jewish customs. He responded with a decisive answer. He was prepared.

There is an interesting epilogue to this story. The morning after this miraculous experience, Paul and Silas were sent word by the magistrates that they were free and should secretly leave the premises. The word had gotten out that these two men of God were party to a major upset in the prison yard. To complicate issues for these magistrates, Paul and Silas were Roman citizens. It was against the law to inflict corporal punishment on a Roman citizen without a trial. Consequently, the magistrates faced the possibility of removal from office for their actions. Paul and Silas were thus brought out of prison and taken to the house of Lydia, where they encouraged the brethren. In the end, God used Paul and Silas's worship in that jail as an opportunity to add to his kingdom.

The Dynamics of Giving and Worship

> Give unto the LORD the glory due unto his name:
> bring an offering, and come into his courts.
>
> Psalm 96:8 KJV

I am a pack rat. That's right, I'm confessing it here and now. I am a pack rat. I am much too sentimental. I collect stuff: books, trains, pictures, recordings, mugs—stuff. Most of the time I try to justify my actions. I need the books—they are my tools. I love model railroading—it's my hobby (never mind that I don't run the trains and I've been hoping since seventh grade to find time to build a large and impressive layout). Pictures in a frame? I don't know why, but I love to frame things, even though it takes me forever to get framed pictures up on the wall. I listen to music—that's my profession. And mugs—I love collecting and drinking from mugs. Yes, I admit it. I am a pack rat.

I don't think I really saw myself as a collector of things until the summer of 1996. We purchased a home, and during the process of moving from one location to the next, friends of ours came over to help. To be honest, we really did have more boxes of books and things than any one family should ever have in a lifetime. After about an hour of unpacking box after box after box, one of our dear friends looked up at me and said, "I have never seen so much stuff in all my life. Vernon, I really believe it is a sin to have all this. And it's just stuff."

After that the Lord began dealing with my heart about spending so much time, money, and energy gathering and collecting things. I realized I had been much more concerned about gathering stuff than giving to others, giving to the kingdom of God, and giving out of a heart full of praise and gratitude. I have come to the conclusion that most of what I collect has very little long-term value for the kingdom of God.

Worship Involves Giving

Worship is about giving—giving to God from a heart of love and adoration, giving of self, giving of talent, giving praise, giving up ambitions, giving strength, giving wealth, and giving up ego. In chapter 6, I outlined God's plan for worship as found in Psalm 96. The third area vital to biblical worship involves giving to the Lord. In fact, true worship can never take place without giving. And one does not sincerely give from a heart of love and devotion to the Lord without worship.

The Bible has a great deal to say about giving. We are commanded to respond to God's goodness by giving back to him (Exod. 25:2; 1 Chron. 29:9; Prov. 3:9). Scripture provides guidelines for giving in the Old and New Testaments (Deut. 16:17; Matt. 6:3; 10:8; Rom. 12:8; 1 Cor. 16:2; 2 Cor. 9:7). We are encouraged to give according to our abilities (Lev. 14:30; Ezra 2:69; Acts 11:29; 2 Cor. 8:12). We are urged to give systematically (1 Cor. 16:2). And we are to give our tithes (Gen. 14:20; 28:22; Mal. 3:10).

Giving is a reflection of our attitude and commitment to praise and worship. Psalm 96:7–9 divides the responsibility of giving to God into three areas.

Giving God Glory

First, genuine worship involves giving God glory. The psalmist says, "Give unto the LORD the glory . . ." (Ps. 96:8 KJV). To do so, we must begin with the part of life that most of us cherish most—our ego, the inner self. If I were in charge, I'd make the first principle of giving apply to money. But that's not the way God works. He is not interested in our stuff. God is much more interested in knowing that our gifts are given as an expression of love and obedience to him. Such giving includes glorifying God for his holiness (Ps. 99:9), love and faithfulness (Ps. 115:1; Isa. 25:1), mercy (Rom. 15:9), wondrous works (Matt. 15:31), judgments (Rev. 14:7), deliverance (Ps. 50:15), and grace (Gal. 2:17–21). The list can certainly go on and on. Why? Because he alone is worthy of praise (2 Sam. 22:4; Rev. 5:12) and is glorified by praise (Ps. 50:23).

The psalmist also says to "give unto the LORD the glory due unto his name" (Ps. 96:8 KJV). Giving God glory and honor due unto his name involves the practice of praise. This means giving God recognition and credit for his majesty, glory, excellence, greatness, holiness, wisdom, power, goodness, mercy, salvation, wonderful works, counsel, and pardon of sin. Why do we praise him? Because he is our hope of glory and the God who answers prayer. He keeps his promises, preserves our life, delivers us from danger, and protects us with his strong arm.

God is glorified when we consciously offer gifts of praise to him. Gifts of praise to Jehovah should be given continually, during all of life, more and more, day and night, day by day, for ever and ever, and from the rising of the sun to its setting. People broaden their horizons and view of a sovereign God when they give him glory. They expand their concept of an eternal God beyond the walls of their small world as they praise. When God's people give glory, they join with the angels (Pss. 103:20; 148:2), saints of the ages (Pss. 30:4; 149:5), children (Ps. 8:2; Matt. 21:16), people of all socioeconomic strata (Ps. 148:11), the small and great (Rev. 19:5), the young and old (Ps. 148:12), and all of creation (Pss. 148:1–10; 145:21; 150:6).

How do we give God glory? The Bible exhorts us to praise God with understanding, with the soul, with the whole heart, with uprightness of heart, with the lips, with the mouth, with joy, with gladness, and with thankfulness. Kenn Mann's song "Everything I Have Is Praise" puts the principle of giving glory into perspective:

> With my heart I'll praise him,
> With my lips I'll glorify his name,
> With my hands I'll serve him forever,
> For my life has been changed.
> Now, everything I have is praise.[1]

I've found that something profoundly joyous begins to happen when saints give glory and praise to God. They begin to show forth more praise, their lives are filled with the spirit of praise (Isa. 61:3), and they render, even under affliction, praise to God (Acts 16:25). As they praise, God gives them the ability and desire to praise even more. They learn how to express their joy by praising God (James 5:13) and then invite others to join in praise (Pss. 34:3; 95:1).

Giving God Strength

The second venue for expressing genuine worship involves giving to the Lord strength. The psalmist says, "Give unto the LORD glory and strength" (Ps. 96:7 KJV). This includes giving to God gifts of labor, work, toil, and effort. It involves giving with a sanctified and non-pretentious heart. The application of this principle is as limitless as the gifts and talents of God's people. To the person with the gifts of time and charity, it might include manning the church nursery during a special program. To the one gifted as a carpenter, the labor of love might involve working around the church, constructing the sets for a Christmas play, or building a platform for use by the choir. To the doctor and nurse with the gift of mercy, a token of love to God might be volunteering to serve on a medical team in a needy or undeveloped country. To the one with talents of administration, a love gift of strength might be heading up an outreach ministry. These are gifts of labor acceptable to God only when given with a contrite and humble spirit. In some cases, these gifts are given and no one in the world, except God, ever knows or gives you credit for doing the good deed. But it doesn't matter who gets the credit when one practices giving back to God and expects nothing in return.

Giving God an Offering

Finally, genuine worship involves giving God an offering. Notice that an offering is the last gift we bring to God. There are two kinds of offerings: (1) an offering of praise and (2) an offering of possessions. Both are needed and are biblical examples of worship.

Giving an offering must be done with a heart full of devotion to the Lord. The motives behind these offerings should be non-pretentious, simple, and honest. I am truly fascinated at the account in 1 Chronicles 29:1–20 of King David gathering offerings for the building of the temple. King David was a warrior and as such was required to shed the blood of other men, an act that disqualified him from physically participating in the building of the temple. So David helped build the temple by giving offerings to the Lord. First Chronicles outlines David's process of giving to God. Paramount to his giving of gifts was an unquestionable affection for God (1 Chron. 29:1–3). He consecrated himself and his people (v. 5) and successfully led God's chosen to give unto the Lord. The Bible states that the leaders of the fathers' houses, leaders of the tribes of Israel, the captains of thousands and of hundreds, with the officers over the king's work, offered willingly. They gave for the work of the house of God. . . . And whoever had precious stones gave them to the treasury of the house of the LORD. . . . Then the people rejoiced, for they had offered willingly, because with a loyal heart they had offered willingly to the LORD; and King David also rejoiced greatly.

1 Chronicles 29:6–9 NKJV

Strategic to this story is their commitment to offer willingly to the Lord (v. 6), to give voluntarily from the heart to the Lord. After giving, they rejoiced (v. 9). David gave his personal fortune to build the temple, a fortune almost immeasurable. Consider this: He gave almost 110 tons of gold and 260 tons of silver. According to today's standard, the total worth of his gift is estimated in the billions of dollars. David gave his very finest, the gold of Ophir. Ophirian gold was the purest and finest in the world. Gifts from God's people were equally stunning. They gave the equivalent of 375 tons of silver, 675 tons of bronze, and 3,750 tons of iron. This too has been estimated at billions of dollars.

David responded to this phenomenal offering by presenting God with sacrifices of praise. Again, he exalted God as Lord. He praised God before the congregation (v. 10). He blessed God for his greatness (vv. 11–12). He acknowledged that all things belong to and come from God (vv. 16–17). Then he prayed that God would help Solomon build the temple (v. 19) and keep his heart loyal to the commandments, testimonies, and statutes of the Lord. He concluded his praise by saying to the assembly, "Praise the LORD your God" (v. 20). They obeyed.

New Testament principles for giving and corporate worship are not at all unlike those practiced by King David. In the New Testament, all giving is from the heart. First, giving is from a sincere heart and "not grudgingly, or of necessity" (2 Cor. 9:7 KJV). Second, giving is with a heart of surrender to God. The apostle Paul commends the Corinthian brethren because they first gave themselves to the Lord (2 Cor. 8:5). Third, giving is with a spirit of unselfishness and sharing (2 Cor. 8:2–4; 9:6), with honor, strength, and without expecting anything in return. Fourth, giving is with a heart of thanksgiving (2 Cor. 9:11–14). By the giving of our stuff, others are blessed, God is glorified, and the gospel of Jesus Christ is advanced.

Worship Is All about Giving to God

Yes, I am a pack rat, but I've learned that we can't take stuff with us when we die. Consider for just one moment what people are going to do with your stuff when you die. Unless you happen to be president of the United States or a famous person, your stuff is going to end up in a yard sale just like mine. And the insult of insults is that the family we leave behind may fuss over our stuff. It's just stuff. And it is stuff that keeps us distracted from worship. God wants us to set our affections on heavenly things, not on the stuff of this world.

Worship is about giving, giving our stuff to God—willingly and in love. Worship is about giving our very best to God. Biblical giving takes place when our devotion to God and his glory compels us to give willingly from the resources of our lives and not due to the expectations of others. We worship when we give glory to God. We worship when we unselfishly give of our strength and labor. We worship when we give from out of the resources with which God has blessed us with "a willing mind . . . according to what one has, and not according to what he does not have" (2 Cor. 8:12 NKJV).

The Dynamics of Prayer and Worship

> Come into his courts. . . . Worship the LORD in the beauty of holiness.
>
> Psalm 96:8–9 KJV

Imagine! A group of first-century Christians, Jewish Christians, gathers in a home for corporate prayer. This is not just any house. This is not just any prayer meeting. This is the home of Mary, the mother of John Mark, the disciple. The meeting is called to pray for Peter. Herod the King has already killed James, the brother of John, and because he saw it pleased the ungodly religious leaders, he has now taken Peter prisoner to await execution. Four squads of soldiers guard Peter. Peter is bound with two chains between two soldiers, and other guards watch the door.

The group prays—together, in one accord. Their friend, mentor, and companion in ministry is in need. Things are critical. Outside of a miracle from God, come morning, Peter will be executed. Constant prayer is offered up to God by the church on Peter's behalf (Acts 12:5). A young girl by the name of Rhoda watches the door. They continue praying.

During the night, God sends an angel to loose Peter's chains. An angel strikes Peter and the chains fall off. The angel commands Peter to get up, put on his clothes and sandals, and follow. Peter is led out of prison, past two groups of guards, through the main gate of the city, and to the street. Peter thinks he is dreaming. When he comes to his senses, he immediately goes to the home of Mary, the mother of John Mark. At that very moment, they are having an extended time of prayer on his behalf, asking God for his release.

Peter knocks on the door. Rhoda answers. She recognizes Peter's voice but because of her gladness forgets to open the door. Running back to her friends, she announces Peter's release. Those praying don't believe her, thinking it is an angel at the door. They apparently return to their prayer. But they finally let Peter in. Even so, the Bible says, "They were astonished" (Acts 12:16). God granted their request even before the prayer meeting had ended.

Principles of Corporate Prayer

I believe God responded in Acts 12 because a group of people were committed to corporate prayer. I wish I could have been a fly on the wall watching everything take place that night. I'm certain I would have learned something mighty important about group prayer.

I'm sure none of us would deny that God moves in hearts, performs his work, protects his children, and brings revival through prayer. Yet, I suspect the average congregation, the average individual professing Christ as Savior spends little time in concentrated, focused corporate prayer. Perhaps our daily actions betray our feelings about participating in prayer as a group. We are not known as a praying people.

I'm sure most of us dismiss the events in Acts 12 as a biblical phenomenon that will not happen in our fast-paced, hurry-and-get-it-done culture. May I suggest the contrary. A worshiping church is always a praying church. A local congregation that devotes significant time to prayer in its corporate services will experience the power of God. God will move in its midst. His power will come upon the members as they seek to minister to fellow believers. God will help that congregation meet the needs of the sick. God will miraculously help them reach the unsaved in their community, launch new and aggressive evangelism campaigns, and build a ministry known for mending the brokenhearted.

How can we spend hours designing worship services, choosing worship songs, selecting worship leaders, and discussing the pros and cons of genuine worship without first giving ourselves to quality time with God? The principles of corporate prayer applied in Acts 12 are even more relevant to worship in our fast-paced, self-consumed, gotta-have-it-now, twenty-first century.

The Priority of Prayer

First, the first-century Christians exhibited the priority of prayer in their corporate worship. The Bible doesn't give any indication as to the service structure, the number of people attending the meeting, or the wording of their prayers. And I'm sure that the desperate need of the hour rather than an intense desire to worship and adore God is what drove these brethren to their knees. Even so, prayer and expressing dependence on God is at the heart of worship. Prayer is God's chosen path for us to reach the throne of grace. In this case, they were absolutely desperate. They needed God to intervene. God responds when people cry out in a spirit of need and dependence.

This congregation in Acts 12 understood the place of prayer. Should we be surprised? The Bible commands it. They were just being obedient. The prophet Isaiah urged the nation of Israel to "seek the LORD while he may be found; call on him while he is near" (Isa. 55:6). Jesus continued the same idea when he said in Matthew 7:7, "Ask and it will be given to you; seek and you will find; knock and the door will be opened to you." The apostle Paul instructed the Philippian brethren, "Do not be anxious about anything, but in everything, by prayer and petition, with thanksgiving, present your requests to God" (Phil. 4:6).

Worship and prayer involve people. God calls people to prayer, not to buildings, well-organized programs, how-to books, or any of a number of other things we see as important to ministry (2 Chron. 7:14). People are given the promises of answered prayer. Intercessory prayers are to be offered up for kings and those in authority (1 Tim. 2:2); ministers (2 Cor. 1:11); all saints (Eph. 6:18; 1 Tim. 2:1); masters and servants (Gen. 24:12–14; Luke 7:2–3); friends and children (Job 42:7–8; Matt. 15:22); the sick (James 5:14); our enemies (Jer. 29:7; Matt 5:44); and fellow countrymen (Rom. 10:1).

I suspect most of us organize and plan our worship ministries with little regard of the need for sustained times in prayer by God's people. Don't you think God must be weary of the way we come and offer a little ditty called the invocation or the pastoral prayer and walk away thinking we've had communion with God? I suspect we rarely get to the heart of important issues in our corporate services because we pray in generalities or minimize the importance of time with God as a group. Perhaps too many of us get restless when a public prayer goes long, when we have to stand too much, or when conversations with God get too personal. We are called, commanded, and commissioned to be people of prayer.

A dimension often overlooked when considering the priority of prayer in corporate worship is the obvious fact that it is most often done as a group—together. That is what these brethren in Acts 12 were doing. The Bible records God's people bowing, lifting up the soul and heart, calling on the name of the Lord, crying to God, beseeching the Lord, seeking God, and making supplication as a group of believers. Corporate worship should include praying specifically for the needs of God's people. Our corporate prayers need to be specific. We should communicate to God the needs of sick patients one by one (and case by case), the concerns of specific missionaries and mission fields (by field and family), and the condition of unsaved individuals (by name). The brothers and sisters in Acts 12 prayed specifically for Peter—as one group, together.

Essential in understanding the priority of prayer in corporate worship is to pray expectantly. I find it most curious that the group in Acts 12 were "astonished" when Peter stood before them, a free man. Obviously, they didn't expect to witness God's answer to prayer, or at least not so soon. Our corporate prayers need to be offered with the same honest conviction we have in our private time with God. We need to believe as a group that God will do what he says. He will answer our prayers. God has promised to "meet all [our] needs according to his glorious riches in Christ Jesus" (Phil. 4:19), grant us the desires of our heart, and hear our prayer.

The Purpose of Prayer

Second, the believers in Acts 12 understood the purpose of prayer in corporate worship. We seek God when we make prayer a strategic part of our corporate worship. Why? Prayer is communication with God. How often in an effort to save time do we ask God during our corporate prayers to "heal all those who are sick," "be with the missionaries around the world," and "help people get saved today?" It is only as we pray strategically—not as a time filler or out of formality or tradition—believing God will do his work that we begin to understand God's purpose for prayer. God wants us to experience the power of corporate communication with him as the Creator. E. M. Bounds was a Methodist preacher born in 1835. He wrote numerous books and became one of America's most intense advocates for prayer in corporate worship. In fact, his two most famous books are *Power through Prayer* and *Purpose in Prayer*. Recently, I had the opportunity to once again read his book *Purpose in Prayer*. He makes the following observation in the first chapter:

> The more praying there is in the world the better the world will be, the mightier the forces against evil everywhere. Prayer, in one phase of its operation, is a disinfectant and preventive. It purifies the air; it destroys the contagion of evil. Prayer is no fitful, short-lived thing. It is no voice crying unheard and unheeded in the silence. It is a voice which goes into God's ear, and it lives as long as God's ear is open to holy pleas, as long as God's heart is alive to holy things.
>
> . . . God shapes the world by prayer. The lips that uttered them may be closed in death, the heart that felt them may have ceased to beat, but the prayers live before God, and God's heart is set on them and prayers outlive the lives of those who uttered them; outlive a generation, outlive an age, outlive a world. That man is most immortal who has done the most and the best praying. They are God's heroes, God's saints, God's servants, God's vicegerents. . . . The prayers of God's saints strengthen the unborn generation against the desolating waves of sin and evil. . . . The prayers of God's saints are the capital stock in Heaven by which Christ carries on his great work upon earth. . . . Earth is changed, revolutionized, angels move on more powerful, more rapid wing, and God's policy is shaped as the prayers are more numerous, more efficient. . . . It is true that the mightiest successes that come to God's cause are created and carried on by prayer. . . . God condi-

tions the very life and prosperity of His cause on prayer. . . . Prayer is the keynote of the most sanctified life, of the holiest ministry. He does the most for God who is the highest skilled in prayer.[1]

May I suggest that corporate prayer provides opportunity for communion (Ps. 96:8–9) and companionship with God. Corporate prayer gives us a platform to offer worship, praise, and adoration to God in public—that continues in private—all the time, without ceasing (1 Thess. 5:17), everywhere (1 Tim. 2:8), day and night (1 Tim. 5:5), and for everything (Phil. 4:6). Corporate prayer is the primary means for a local church to enjoy continued blessings from God (Exod. 20:24; Matt. 6:33).

The Promise and Power of Prayer

Third, the miracle of Acts 12 is evidence of the promise and power of prayer in corporate worship. God promises to hear and respond to public prayer (2 Chron. 7:14). He promises his blessings when people join together in prayer (Exod. 20:24). In Matthew 18:19, Jesus promises answers to prayer. We can and must depend on God to do what he says he will do.

In the book *Fresh Wind, Fresh Fire,* Jim and Carol Cymbala give testimony of the priority, promise, and power of prayer in their ministry at the Brooklyn Tabernacle. Jim gives scores of examples of how God uses prayer in the services. First, the entire congregation participates in extended prayer times during the regular services. It is a vital part of worship. Second, a host of people gathers in another room during the morning services. They worship God and intercede on behalf of the pastor. Third, Tuesday evenings are devoted entirely to worshiping and praying. The Cymbalas believe this once-a-week meeting is the power behind their ministry. The prayer time begins with energetic and intense songs of worship and praise. Then the entire congregation spends an extended time on their knees simply worshiping God, offering petitions to God, and participating in intercessory prayer. What Jim and Carol Cymbala are doing is practicing the power of prayer. Week after week, they witness the wonder of God's work through answered prayer. Lives are changed, homes restored, broken hearts mended. They praise God and watch him meet spiritual, emotional, and financial needs.

The Process of Prayer

Fourth, Acts 12 illustrates something of the process of prayer in corporate worship. While nothing is specifically stated in this passage about the manner and structure of the prayer service by the brethren, it is obvious some type of process was executed. For example, some prayed while others watched (Rhoda tending the door), they were in constant prayer (v. 5), and they gathered together as believers (v. 12).

Multitudes of other Scripture passages shed light on the process. Most often, the process begins with our personal and public motives. Consider this: Prayers are to be offered up in the Holy Spirit (Eph. 6:18); in faith (Matt. 21:22; James 1:6); in full assurance of faith (Heb. 10:22); in a forgiving spirit (Matt. 6:12); with the heart (Jer. 29:13); with the whole heart (Ps. 119:58); with the preparation of the heart (Job 11:13); with a sincere heart (Heb. 10:22); with the spirit and the mind (1 Cor. 14:15; John 4:22–24); with confidence in God (Pss. 56:9; 86:7; 1 John 5:14); with deliberation (Eccles. 5:2); with holiness (1 Tim. 2:8); with humility (2 Chron. 7:14; 33:12); with truth (Ps. 145:18; John 4:24); with the desire to be heard (Neh. 1:6; Pss. 17:1; 55:1–2; 61:1); and with a desire to be answered (Pss. 27:7; 102:2; 108:6; 143:1).

In chapter 1, I wrote about a remarkable church led by an equally remarkable pastor in Oklahoma. Sometime in the mid-1980s, the Lord began dealing with this pastor about his public and private prayer life. This dear brother promised God that he would spend an hour a day in private prayer. He committed himself and the church to significant times of worship through prayer during the public services. Over the years, God has used the prayers from this congregation to advance the kingdom over and over again. The congregation has learned by example that the prayers of a righteous man are powerful.

Significant time during the regularly scheduled Sunday morning service is given to prayer—and without apology. Sunday services are from 10:30 A.M. to 12:00. The members of the congregation spend approximately twenty to twenty-five minutes intensely expressing praise and worshiping the Lord, mostly through song and Scripture reading. The pastor usually limits his sermons to approximately twenty-five to thirty minutes (although that is not a hard and fast rule). The remaining time is spent in public prayer.

Over the years, this special prayer time has become the focal point of the service. People walk away from the morning worship talking about God and how he answers prayer. The church stands as a testimony of God's provisions through answered prayer. On many occasions, people publicly confess sin, ask the congregation to join in praying for lost loved ones, witness the miracle work of God's healing, praise God for restoring families, and cry out for God to mend broken hearts. This group can trace hundreds of miracles directly to their prayer time.

The special times of corporate prayer influence the pastor's sermons as well. He preaches with power and conviction. There is a sense of freshness when he speaks. It is obvious when he stands before the people that he has a word from God, and the people follow the pastor's lead.

I learned something about the process of corporate prayer during my time with this pastor. Since those days,

I too have nurtured and developed a seven-step pattern for public prayer:

1. Exaltation of God is first. Exalt and brag about God for his works and marvelous acts. It is during this time that I bless God for his mighty wonders, creation, stars, sky, life, and everything that he has done. I endeavor, with all the sincerity of my spirit, to lift up the name of Jesus.
2. Next, give praise to God (Ps. 66:17). This is a time of giving God glory for his provisions, redemption, salvation, work in the church, and so on.
3. Express thanks and appreciation to God for everything (Phil. 4:6; Col. 4:2). Give thanks for obvious things such as health, food, and normal provisions, which we often take for granted. This is followed by more personal words of thanks for such things as family, job, church, and friends.
4. The fourth area of corporate prayer includes confession and repentance of sin (Neh. 1:4, 7; Dan. 9:4–11). Pray about things that seem to capture your attention and hinder fellowship with God. I usually mention such sins as pride, ego, wrong motives, and so on.
5. Public praise is fifth. Praise God for answered prayer, provision of needs, or public responses to God for his goodness.
6. Offer prayers of intercession. I sometimes follow the pattern in the Bible, which includes but is not limited to prayer for kings (1 Tim. 2:2); all in authority (including the president of the country) (1 Tim. 2:2); those in spiritual leadership (2 Cor. 1:11; Phil. 1:19); all saints (Eph. 6:18); everyone (1 Tim. 2:1); masters and servants (Gen. 24:12–14; Luke 7:2–3); children (Gen. 17:18; Matt. 15:22); friends and fellow countrymen (Job 42:8; Rom. 10:1); the sick (Num. 12:13; James

5:14); persecutors, enemies among whom we dwell, and those who envy us (Jer. 29:7; Matt. 5:44). I then take the prayer requests given by those in the congregation and offer intercession on behalf of the people.
7. Finally, offer petitions. Ask God to provide and simply bring each desire of the heart to the Lord.

The Practicality of Prayer

The fifth and final lesson we can learn from Acts 12 is that prayer in corporate worship should be practical. The desperate needs of a beloved brother is what drove the Christians to their knees in Acts 12. They had witnessed the executions of James and other fellow believers. They did not want to see that happen again. They focused on important issues. They continued in prayer with persistence and purpose.

Keeping corporate prayer practical and focused on worship may be a difficult challenge, but consistent, faithful, and purpose-driven prayer is the source of power for worshiping believers.

A local church or fellowship is never the same after its members capture a vision for and practice corporate prayer. I encourage you to make whatever sacrifice necessary to provide extended times of prayer during the regularly scheduled services at your church. Keep in mind that God's people worship and communicate with God through prayer. Don't allow Satan to rob you of critical and precious moments in prayer.

Prayer Is at the Heart of Biblical Worship

Recently, I was asked to serve as a guest worship leader for the Sunday morning and evening services at a nearby church. The pastor asked me to structure the worship for both services. Such a task usually involves selecting songs and Scripture, organizing the order of services, deciding on how we are going to express worship, and finding appropriate personnel to help in the presentation. This I did.

The Sunday morning service went well. Good pacing. Good choice of songs. Good balance between old and new. Good use of Scripture. Great congregational participation. And, of course, plenty of time for the sermon. The pastor was pleased and could not say enough good things about the service.

On Sunday night there was unusually good audience participation. Good use of Scripture. Good use of old and new songs. And during this service three separate times were designated for corporate prayer: the first time for exaltation of God, the second for praise of God's mighty work, the third to express love and adoration to God. Each period of prayer was preceded by Scripture and followed by spontaneous singing. It was truly a moving and heart-searching time.

At the conclusion of the service, the pastor asked to have a word with me. He said, "Vernon, don't you think we had too much prayer tonight?" He continued by expressing his disappointment that the Sunday night service did not have the same level of excitement as the morning service. "I just don't think our people are known in this community as a praying church."

His statements about the evening service and prayer give me pause even to this day. This dear brother, deeply concerned about leading a fellowship known for its "ministry of excitement," did not understand that the power for ministry comes from the time his congregation worships in prayer.

I'm of the conviction that a worshiping congregation will always be a praying congregation. Worship of God through prayer begins as we practice prayer in our own lives first. Then we take time to lead and teach our people on Sunday mornings to join hands and lift their voices to heaven. You see, God is praised when we pray (Ps. 66:17); we are commanded to pray (Isa. 55:6; Matt. 7:7; Phil. 4:6); God hears and answers prayer (Pss. 65:2; 99:6; Isa. 58:9); the prayer of a righteous person is powerful and effective (James 5:16); and our prayers are to be offered through Christ (John 14:13–14; 15:16; 16:23–25; Eph. 2:18; Heb. 10:19).

I can't imagine the brothers and sisters in Acts 12 doubting for even one minute the effectiveness of corporate prayer—not after their experience with Peter's release from prison. I'm equally sure they never questioned their identity as a praying church. And I am convinced their commitment to prayer was rewarded by the power of God moving across their fellowship. Perhaps they were never the same after Peter knocked on their door that night. They had witnessed the power of the Holy Spirit in response to their worship and prayer. And even though they were admittedly astonished and perhaps doubted just a little when they saw Peter at the door, their testimony of faith was evidenced in their constant commitment to prayer. They overcame the hindrances to prayer, devoted serious time to prayer, committed themselves to pray together, and in the end reaped the benefit.

The Dynamics of Preaching and Worship

> For the preaching of the cross . . . is the power of God.
>
> 1 Corinthians 1:18 KJV

It was a cool night in the fall of 1999. A group of roughly one thousand educators, pastors, musicians, college administrators, and friends met together in the ministry center of the Christian college where I teach to celebrate the home going of a wonderfully gifted mother, wife, and coworker.

My wife and I got to the meeting early and sat quietly while the organist played a series of hymns, gospel songs, and praise and worship favorites. As I sat pondering the coming events, my eyes glanced across the program for the evening. It read: The Graduation Service for Helen Drullinger. Graduation service! It was obvious this was not going to be an ordinary memorial service.

A few minutes later, Dave Drullinger, husband of the deceased, entered the building with a group of family and close friends. A pastor began the service by praying and reminding us as a congregation that we were gathered to worship. He asked God to enable us to worship him. We sang the hymns "Great Is Thy Faithfulness" and "Like a

River Glorious." The college choir sang the old Southern gospel favorite "I Bowed on My Knees and Cried Holy." A soloist sang Carol Cymbala's song "He's Been Faithful." We watched a video of Helen and Dave Drullinger's life. We rejoiced and witnessed God's blessings on their long and fruitful ministry together.

In spite of more than eighteen months of uncertainty, chemotherapy, hospital visits, mounting expenses, and finally the passing of one dearly loved and admired, one by one, family members and friends gave testimony of God's grace and goodness. It was a sweet time full of precious moments and memories.

What I remember most about this memorial service, Helen's graduation ceremony, was the power of the spoken Word. After the singing, Scripture reading, sharing of testimonies, and moments spent reflecting on the life of Helen and Dave Drullinger's ministry together, Dave got up and preached. He continued worshiping as he preached. He said, "You know, my wife and I debated the appropriateness of me delivering this message. We concluded that I was the only one who could tell the story of how God is good all the time. In fact, the chorus 'God Is so Good' became our theme song. Night and day we sang to God of his goodness to us."

Taking his text from Psalm 73:23–28, Dave read:

> You hold me by my right hand.
> You guide me with your counsel,
>   and afterward you will take me into glory.
> Whom have I in heaven but you?
>   And earth has nothing I desire besides you.
> My flesh and my heart may fail,
>   but God is the strength of my heart
>   and my portion forever.
> Those who are far from you will perish;
>   you destroy all who are unfaithful to you.

But as for me, it is good to be near God.
I have made the Sovereign LORD my refuge;
I will tell of all your deeds.

For more than thirty minutes, Dave stood and told us of God's goodness. He said, "God is not the author of disease—he is the source of all healing; God is not the author of suffering—he is the source of all comfort; God is not the author of sin—he is the source of redemption; God is not the author of death—he is the source of life; and God is not the author of sorrow—he is the source of hope."

God gave Helen the wisdom to know and recognize God's goodness. He gave Dave the grace and courage to preach about God's goodness during the deepest, darkest moment of his life. That night, Dave and Helen presented God a genuine sacrifice of praise and worship. Dave worshiped as he preached, and we worshiped through his preaching. Dave was fixed on the wonder of God, worshiping the entire time he shared the gospel, clearly speaking words of peace, rest, and assurance.

Preaching and Worship

It has long been my conviction that the time spent singing, praying, reading Scripture, sharing testimony, and giving gifts is not a preliminary before the *really important* part of the service, the sermon. Rather, corporate worship begins with the first moments of singing or proclamation of Scripture and continues through the sermon and to the benediction. As preachers, we worship as we declare the Word of God to our congregations. As corporate worshipers sitting in the pew, we worship as we listen to the Word of God. As individuals, we worship when we feed on the Word of God and apply it to daily living.

All of us have no doubt listened to sermons given by persons not engaged in worship. A man of God can preach without worshiping—and the Word will not return void. But a man of God truly experiencing the joy of worshiping in spirit and in truth will never preach the gospel without worshiping.

How do we know when sermons become sacrifices of worship? What translates the words of a sermon from intellectual truth and facts about God to genuine worship? And what is it about preaching the Word that captivates a congregation and leads the members to worship?

First, preaching becomes a sacrifice of praise when it exalts the Person of truth. God is the Person of truth, and when sermons exalt him as such, preaching praises the Almighty, and we worship. Over and over Dave Drullinger proclaimed the truth that God is good even when things seem bad. Never did he exalt himself, brag about the good deeds he performed as a care giver to a dying wife, or seek in any way to give himself glory. Rather, Dave told about the Person of truth and of God's work among people during times of serious need. In so doing, he led us in worship. He exalted Christ and moved the congregation to do the same.

Second, preaching engages people in worship when it explains and expounds the gospel of Jesus Christ. When the gospel is explained, God's people are edified, the unsaved are evangelized, and the truth of his Word pierces the soul and spirit (Heb. 4:12). Scripture provides precedent for the presentation of the gospel: Luke 2:10–11 presents the gospel as good tidings of great joy for all people. The truth of the gospel as seen in the person of Christ is foretold in Isaiah 41:27; 52:7; 61:1–3; and Mark 1:15. The gospel is preached (Heb. 4:2); exhibits the grace of God (Acts 14:3); and provides an avenue for people to understand the glory of God (2 Cor. 4:4, 6). Life and immortality are brought to light by Jesus through the gospel (2 Tim. 1:10). In Romans 1:16, 1 Corinthians 1:18, and 1 Thessalonians 1:5, the gospel is called the power of God unto salvation, and in 1 Peter 1:25 and Revelation 14:6 it is called everlasting. The gospel was preached by Christ (Matt. 4:23; Mark 1:14), and those of us in the ministry have an obligation as good stewards to preach the gospel as well (1 Cor. 9:17). The gospel is the Word of God (1 Thess. 2:13) that presents Christ as the preeminent one (Col. 1:15–18); and the source of grace (Acts 14:3; 20:32); salvation (Acts 13:26); reconciliation (2 Cor. 5:19); truth (Eph. 1:13; James 1:18); faith (Rom. 10:8); and life (John 14:6).

At the heart of biblical preaching that engages people in biblical worship is the presentation of the gospel of Jesus Christ. The gospel itself is the power of God that edifies and encourages. We worship as we listen to the preached Word of God.

Third, we worship God through the Word when we extol the power and wonder of God. We extol God when we commend, compliment, laud, applaud, eulogize, acclaim, or celebrate his greatness. My friend Dave Drullinger extolled God in his sermon as he gave God all the glory and credit for being "good all the time."

Warren Wiersbe makes the following observation about the power of the preached Word when applied to individual needs:

> The Bible is written for the heart as well as the head; otherwise it would not be saturated as it is with poetry, symbolism, and just about every literary device that captures the imagination and emotions. After all, preaching deals with real life, the life in the Word and life in the pew; and it takes imagination to build that bridge from an ancient book to a modern need. . . . When Jesus wanted to help people stop worrying, He did not give a lecture on Hebrew and Greek words. Instead, He talked about birds, flowers, and robbers. He appealed to the imagination of His listeners, gripped their hearts, and then instructed their minds.[1]

Biblical preaching is preaching that provides opportunity for the preacher and the listener to enter into worship. Unlike anything else, when we listen to preaching that extols God and explains the gospel, the Holy Spirit reassures us as listeners (worshipers in the pew) of the promises of God. He brings peace (Eph. 6:15), produces hope (Col. 1:23), and there is fullness of blessing (Rom. 15:29). As the preacher commends, compliments, applauds, and celebrates God, the Holy Spirit settles and calms the heart, scatters the clouds brought by anxious moments, helps us to focus on the all-sufficiency of our sovereign God, provides instruction in righteousness, and clearly illuminates Christ as the only hope for eternity.

Fourth, we worship God through the Word when Christ is exalted as the source of redemption. Dave Drullinger exalted Christ by saying that "God is not the author of sin—he is the source of redemption." When we preach, we share the mystery of the gospel (Eph. 6:19). The Bible tells us that the Holy Spirit moved on men to write his thoughts and wonders (Acts 1:16; Heb. 3:7; 2 Peter 1:21). We have received his Word through the inspiration of a sovereign God (2 Tim. 3:16). God sent his Son to reconcile us to himself. When we preach redemption, we preach the plan and purpose of God. Scripture gives testimony that God provides his Word for the purpose of bringing humans unto himself. He has given us the Scriptures from his own heart.

Is it any wonder that when we read and hear the Word of God, we are prone to worship? Is it any wonder that when we are fed from the Word of God, we worship? The Scriptures are full and sufficient and an unerring guide (Prov. 6:23; 2 Peter 1:12–21). This same Word of God is able to make us wise and show us salvation through faith in Christ Jesus (2 Tim. 3:15).

Some years ago, the college where I teach hosted a summit on church music ministry. More than 130 pastors, ministers of music, music publishers, Christian artists, and music educators met on our campus for the purpose of discussing the challenges facing us in the area of worship.

On the last night of the summit, we gathered in the college chapel with the entire student body for a worship service. We opened up the service with a medley of hymns, including "Hallelujah, What a Savior!" Our hearts were stirred, God was exalted, and we worshiped as we were moved by the power of the text:

> Man of Sorrows! What a name,
> For the Son of God who came
> Ruined sinners to reclaim!
> Hallelujah, what a Savior!

At the conclusion of the hymn we stood in silence as a young nursing student from Oregon quoted from memory the entire book of 1 Peter. Never before or since have I witnessed an audience so spellbound by the sheer wonder of hearing God's spoken Word. We listened as she proclaimed Peter's reminder to endure through persecution, glorify God, lay up treasures in heaven, and live as God's obedient children. The Holy Spirit used the Word of God to speak to our hearts with peace, purpose, and power. People wept as she spoke. Others raised their hands in praise to God. When she finished, no one uttered a sound. It was as if we responded to the spoken Word by worshiping in silence. The Word of God was spoken. Jesus was presented as the one true, eternal redeemer. And we worshiped.

Finally, preaching the Word engages us in worship when we are edified by the promises of the gospel. At the conclusion of Dave Drullinger's memorial sermon, he presented us with a series of promises about the Word of God. We worshiped God as Dave reminded us that God is good—all the time—

and that God's Word is faithful and true. We were encouraged, edified, and refreshed as we worshiped together. Consider this: The Bible is described as flawless (Ps. 12:6; Prov. 30:5); true (Ps. 119:160; John 17:17); perfect (Ps. 19:7); radiant (Ps. 19:8); precious (Ps. 19:10); and living and active (Heb. 4:12). It is provided for our instruction (Rom. 15:4) and intended for use by all nations (Rom. 16:26). It is designed for regenerating (James 1:18; 1 Peter 1:23); preserving life (Ps. 119:50, 93); illuminating (Ps. 119:130); and reviving the soul (Ps. 19:7). The gospel makes wise the simple (Ps. 19:7); and produces faith (John 20:31); hope (Ps. 119:49; Rom. 15:4); and obedience (Deut. 17:19–20). It cleanses the heart (John 15:3; Eph. 5:26) and keeps us from destructive paths (Ps. 17:4). No wonder lives are changed when the Word of God is preached. We are prone to worship when we hear the spoken Word, which illuminates, revives, produces faith, and keeps us from destructive paths.

Preaching from an Overflow of Worship

In chapter 5, I told how my best friend, Jonathan Thigpen, and I met in college. I told how God opened doors for us to partner in evangelism. God has blessed both of us in ministry these past twenty-five years. We still enjoy opportunities to get together and fellowship in ministry.

About four years ago, Jonathan called me to say he had been diagnosed with Lou Gehrig's disease. I was stunned. He was optimistic. Since then, he has experienced continued deterioration of his muscles. He now walks with braces and has lost the use of one arm.

He still preaches with power and conviction. Since the diagnosis of this disease, his preaching has developed a richness and depth that I've not seen or experienced before. It is as if his preaching is an extension of his own worship time with God. When he speaks, there are few wasted words, few moments of humor, and a renewed sense of eternity. He speaks as one having authority and focus.

Last March, Jonathan asked me to join him in a series of revival meetings in south Georgia. It was a wonderful time of renewed fellowship with friends and incredible worship services. On one night of the meeting, Jonathan preached a powerful sermon. In the concluding moments of the sermon, he made the following statement:

> I have a terminal disease. And so do you. I just know what is going to get me. I've found that when it is all said and done that all anyone can depend on is this [holding up his Bible]. I've found that even when the water runs deep, you can depend on the Word to get you through. And that when you stand on the truth of God's Word, it is always solid at the bottom.

Jonathan understands something about worship and the Word of God that most of us will never know this side of heaven. He understands how to worship while feeding on the Word. He is living out the truth that the Bible is the Word of God (Luke 11:28; Heb. 4:12). God is teaching him firsthand that the Bible, the revealed law, statutes, and judgments of God (Exod. 24:3–4; Deut. 4:5, 14), can be trusted and are full of promises on which we can depend. Jonathan understands that when we worship God in truth, we will desire to hear and obey his Word (Matt. 7:24; Luke 11:28; James 1:22). God is allowing Jonathan the privilege of turning his study into a sanctuary of praise.

Warren Wiersbe puts into perspective the worship experienced when hearing and preaching the Word:

> The kind of preaching the unsaved world needs to hear is not manufactured from books. . . . You do

not "build" a sermon by borrowing pieces from Spurgeon, Billy Sunday [and I might add Billy Graham, Bill Hybels, Rick Warren, Warren Wiersbe, and any other preacher], the morning newspaper, and the notes in your study Bible. A message from God is the living consequence of a vital meeting with God during which you worshiped Him and permitted His truth to set fire to your soul. When the minister's study turns into a sanctuary, a holy of holies, then something transforming will happen as the Word of God is proclaimed. As our lives are transformed, the church will be transformed, and this will open the way for us to reach out to a lost world that knows not God.[2]

Dave Drullinger and Jonathan Thigpen both preach from the overflow of a genuine worship of God. They understand the living consequence of a vital meeting with God during which they worship God. No wonder we worshiped as Dave preached. No wonder the power of the Holy Spirit came upon the audience that night when we attended the summit on church music ministry. No wonder my friend Jonathan can stand firm on the promises of the Word of God. God and his Word were given their rightful place of exaltation, wonder, majesty, and worship.

Thirteen

The Dynamics of People and Worship

And when he had saluted them, he declared particularly what things God had wrought . . . by his ministry.

Acts 21:19 KJV

I want to take this opportunity to focus on one of the most important aspects of corporate worship. People. I want to share with you straight from my heart. I've been a minister of music/worship leader for more than twenty-five years. The Lord has given me a rich and wonderful life. Along the journey, the Lord has used people, circumstances, educational and ministry opportunities, and various successes and disappointments to mold and shape me. The Lord has taken me as a severely wounded soldier and nurtured me back to a place of productive service (see chapter 1). He has opened incredible doors of opportunity, miraculously supplied needs, and proven himself victorious over and over again. I've stood by the side of dying loved ones, rejoiced at the birth of children, and provided music and encouragement at important times of need. I've seen the Lord honor feeble attempts at ministry, and I've witnessed his marvelous work when my elaborate plans for grand and majestic presentations have failed. Through it all, I've learned two principles: (1) God uses people, and (2) God always supplies my needs.

Ministering to a New Generation

With disbelief, I look back on the events, various social movements, changes in politics and governmental strategies, and shifts in religious paradigms that have taken place during my life. Below is a list of people, events, court decisions, tragedies, accomplishments, and changes. Each is significant to American culture. Each conjures up an emotion or memory in the mind of most Americans. Consider how you might identify with the following:

Popular music: Elvis, the king of rock 'n' roll; the Beatles; the Mamas and the Papas; Otis Redding; Woodstock; the Rolling Stones; the Grateful Dead; Jim Croce; Frank Sinatra

Politics: prayer in school; prayer out of school; Vietnam; Watergate; the Bay of Pigs; the end of communism as we know it; the resignation of a president; the impeachment of another president

Tragedies: John F. Kennedy's and Martin Luther King's assassinations; the AIDS epidemic; the Oklahoma City bombing; the Columbine school shooting

Technology: personal computers; cellular phones; the Internet; laser surgery; musical instrument digital interfacing (MIDI); communication by means of satellite; fiber optics; e-mail; fax machines; videotapes; CDs

Methods in ministry have changed too. Remember the Jesus Movement, the early youth musicals, the introduction of Scripture songs, and singing to overheads?

Over the years, I've seen hearts broken by sin mended and renewed by the power of the Holy Spirit. I've watched men of the gospel fall, never to stand before the public to minister again, marriages crumble, children rebel, and people withdraw from the warmth of a church body because we would not (or could not) reach out in a critical time of need.

What do I see as I look back over the past years? How are we going to minister effectively to a new generation? How do we teach this new generation to worship and still maintain effective communication with the aging in the church? Consider the following.

First, we are called to minister in a changing world. All of us—worship leaders, church administrators, ministers of music, pastors, Christian laypersons—are faced with new challenges: People have new and unique needs because they live in a changing world. Our values are changing. We live in a postmodern, secular society that confuses spirituality with spiritual truth and aesthetics with corporate worship. Our society, business practices, finances, norms—our lives in every respect—are changing. We are a needy people. We have emotional, spiritual, intellectual yearnings that must be fulfilled. Our concept of trust is changing. Yet, God made human beings with the natural desire to worship. No matter how much things change in this world, the hunger in our hearts is to know God and worship. Therefore, we must find a way to minister in this world.

Second, there is a renewed emphasis on excellence. The word *excellence* is used more than ever. It is the buzzword of our decade. Businesses talk about it. Colleges advertise their commitment to it. Societies in general are establishing new norms for excellence. Ministries of all sorts are claiming excellence in all things. Worship ministries face the challenge of developing communication avenues with excellence.

Third, we live in an era of social and spiritual upheaval. We are an overworked, overcommitted, spiritually malnourished society. We often base decisions and aspirations on hedonistic ambitions, desires, and peer acceptance. We have reared a generation that knows more about video games, the latest television sitcom, and its favorite fad in clothing than God, church, or the home. We are a nation in desperate need of direction.

Fourth, we cannot help but be saddened by missed opportunities. Those of us who have done ministry for a number of years can look to the past and see squandered potential and overlooked opportunities. Sometimes we missed opportunities because we didn't have the proper resources. More often, we failed to capture the vision of reaching out to those around us. Some of us missed opportunities because we are poor managers of our time and resources. Whatever the reason, we missed opportunities to discover our own potential and the potential within others.

Fifth, we must seek new ways to minister. Changes in technology, improvements in communication, social challenges around us, cultural metamorphosis, economic shifts, and ecclesiastical nuances of this century all present new and exciting challenges for ministry. Ministry is also threatened by the changing norms in our society, shifts in educational and cultural paradigms, and a perceived void of absolutes. People just like you and me are reaching out, seeking ways to meet their inner need to worship. God is moving and his church is responding.

People are spiritually hungry, wanting to know God. Masses of people are seeking new and creative ways to worship the Almighty. Opportunities for ministry are unfolding before our eyes as never before. New and exciting avenues for communicating the gospel are emerging. Social changes among people groups are opening doors of opportunity for presenting the gospel in regions once closed to the truth. Now, it is time for ministers of music, worship leaders, pastors, and congregations across this great land to evaluate their ministries, redefine their purposes, and launch aggressive programs to teach, train, evangelize, edify, and promote the work of Christ.

Ministering Corporate Worship

In the Old Testament, priestly responsibilities included ministering sacrifices on behalf of the people to the Lord. Priests were given the opportunity to minister to God and to God's people. Those of us given the responsibility of leading worship in the twenty-first century need to accept the task of providing ministry (serving, loving, giving gifts, and so on) to God and on behalf of our congregations. Likewise, we need to see that we are ministering to God's people as we worship God together. I purposely use the phrase "ministering worship" to describe this joyous privilege. It defines the service (ministry) that I do unto the Lord (worship, love, exalt, and adore him) and that which God allows me to provide for and to his people (leading, teaching, and practicing principles of worship with the congregation).

We as worship leaders in the twenty-first century need to focus on the purpose for which we have been called—to engage God's people in worship. We need to develop and refine our worship ministries and endeavor to include all of God's people in worship—young and old alike. We need to capture a vision for teaching and admonishing, instructing and training, and nurturing and maturing people as worshipers. This process is what I call ministering worship. How can we be successful in ministering worship to and with our congregations?

Focus on People Not Programs

To be successful in ministering corporate worship, we need to focus on people not programs. God calls us to work with people, and the Spirit of God indwells people. We have the unique responsibility as worship leaders to lead people to the throne of God through praise and worship. We have the privilege of teaching people how to develop a dynamic relationship with God. We have the joyous opportunity of encouraging, edifying, and energizing congregations to worship.

I remember hearing a radio preacher talk about important things to remember in life. One of his principles dealt with the essentials of working with people. "After all," he said, "Jesus died for people." I say a hearty amen. Jesus died for people, and we are called to minister to people. Maybe we need to be reminded that corporate worship does not take place without people.

It is easy for us to plan, write, organize, and structure elaborate worship activities and ministry opportunities for people and never really touch lives. But people need for us to have a warm heart, gentle touch, sincere interest, and genuine regard for their needs. Our responsibility is to minister to the people of God.

How do we do this? *First, those of us ministering to God's people must cultivate a dynamic relationship with people.* We need to see them as "the vineyard" to which God has called us to minister. We must know our people—know what they like. Each culture, denomination, local church, church-related group (such as a camp or para-church organization), Bible study group, and congregation has its own dynamic. This is especially true when it comes to music preferences and worship practices. To superimpose a personal preference on a congregation or worship group without regard to preestablished practices, likes or dislikes, and norms may render our ministry ineffective.

Second, be genuine. We are fooling ourselves if we believe that people don't know when pastors and worship leaders are acting like they appreciate a certain type of music, ministry approach, or worship philosophy when in reality they don't. Make a point to learn and appreciate what your people like. If you are genuine, people will still love and appreciate you even when they disagree with your approach to or concept of ministry.

Third, establish a common trust between you and the people with whom you minister. People need to know and the minister of worship needs to show that there are no hidden agendas. As a leader of worship, you must have your congregation's best interest at heart. Love and respect your people. Be honest in your approach to ministry. Endeavor to consistently meet their spiritual needs. Be an encourager. Make sure to tell those who help you lead worship that they are important to your ministry. Express appreciation to them for their work and always encourage them to trust God to help them as they grow and develop their abilities as worship leaders.

Focus on Potential Not Problems

To be successful in ministering corporate worship, we must focus on potential not problems. It has been said, "I could have a great ministry if it weren't for the people." Those of us in leadership positions will never realize success without people (more about that in the next two chapters). We are called to work with people. Too often we focus on the talent resources we don't have and fail to train and disciple the very people God has entrusted to our care. We need to remember that God takes ordinary people with ordinary talents and abilities and uses them to do extraordinary things. And God is performing this unique miracle in the lives of his people every day of the year. The people God gives us to work with are our partners in doing and completing his work. Often God simply wants us to help people recognize their giftedness. He gives us as worship leaders the responsibility to help people discover their own potential. Once that is accomplished, we need to nurture their gifts, provide opportunities for them to learn, encourage them to dream and grow in their walk with Christ, and help them develop their own musical, ministry, and leadership potential.

Focus on Being Practical Not Philosophical

To be successful in ministering corporate worship, we must focus on being practical not philosophical. Being practical involves setting realistic goals and boundaries for ministries. In order to do so, ask youself the following questions.

Scripture

- What does the Bible say?
- Are there scriptural mandates for me to follow?
- Are there clear and definite guidelines already established in the Bible?
- Is there a correlation between what I want to do and what the Bible tells me to do?

Culture

- How does my concept of ministry fit within the culture or cultures of the group to whom I'm called to minister?
- Are there any social implications of my approach to music and worship?
- What are the long-range effects of my ministry approach?
- How will I deal with those who oppose what I do?

Style of Music

- Is the style of music I prefer acceptable to the majority of the people, or am I limiting my ministry to a small group?
- Will the music communicate to the entire group?
- Can I be eclectic and still minister, or am I trying to be all things to all people?
- Is what I do (or choose not to do) compromising the work God has called me to?
- Whom am I seeking to reach?

People

- Do I have the human resources necessary to make the ministry successful?
- Are the people willing to participate?
- How do I encourage people to discover and develop their God-given potential?
- Am I using people's talents and gifts to advance the kingdom of God?

Physical Resources

- What kind of financial and physical resources do I have?
- How can I best meet the needs of people with the physical resources God has given to me?
- Is the building adequate?
- Do I have enough music, or do I need to make strategic purchases?
- What kind of supplies do I need?

Ministry Outcomes

- What is the desired outcome of this ministry?
- What is my role in making this worship ministry successful?

- Is the ministry going to have a positive effect on my community and culture?
- Am I keeping eternal values in view?
- Am I using my talents and gifts most effectively?

Focus on the Person of Worship—Jesus!

Flee from the temptation to build a worship ministry on ego or pride. I recently read an ad inviting people to hear "the all-star worship and praise band" at a well-known Christian conference. I wonder how God looks on our presentation of worship with an "all-star" cast. I'm sure he is not at all impressed. In order for worship to be meaningful and most effective, hearts must be focused on Jesus as "the Star." In reality, he is the only star and the only one deserving our attention, honor, and focus. Do not allow the worship order, personalities of leaders, or manner of presentation to become the focus of the service. How does one keep focus on Jesus? Here are a few suggestions:

The Presentation of Worship

- Flow from one moment to the next with very few announcements and extra talking.
- Make sure each element (music, drama, Scripture) fits into the worship flow.
- Make all announcements before the worship begins or at the end of the service.

The Music

- Select songs everyone can sing—don't allow the song selections to draw attention to the worship leaders.
- When teaching new songs, teach only one or maybe two in a service. The introduction of too many new songs in one service distracts from the worship flow and often inhibits genuine worship.

- Endeavor to keep song services fresh, well organized, and focused on Jesus—select songs that present Christ and his wisdom, wonder, and work.

The Message

- Keep all comments focused on the Lord, his work and power, and his leadership in the lives of people.
- Keep all personal testimonies focused on what God is doing within the lives of individuals.
- Publicly express gratitude to God for the good things he does for and within the congregation.
- Keep all drama, readings, and Scripture presentations short, to-the-point, and focused on only one or two important doctrinal or scriptural principles.

The Musicians

- Make sure solos or duet presentations do not draw attention to the people doing the singing.
- Encourage your musicians to search their hearts (Psalm 50; 139)—all hearts must focus on the things of the Lord. God is the one being exalted, not the singers and players.
- Remember, worship is a team effort, but Jesus is the only star!

Leading God's People in Worship

Leading God's people in worship is not a choice between being traditional or contemporary. It most often involves being sensitive to needs and seeking the Holy Spirit to make practical application of truth in people's lives.

Over the last twenty-five years, I've learned that working with and alongside people is crucial to successful ministry. The relationships I establish with God's people, my disposition, my respect for those in authority, my genuine love for people, and my belief in others' ability and potential are what help me lead. I can put together large and successful worship programs, gather thousands at rallies and other events, help run successful fund-raising campaigns, and more, but what people are going to remember more than anything is the kind of relationships I have with them. That means respecting other people's opinions, guarding my character and integrity, loving people when they seem unlovable, and keeping the big picture of ministry in view.

Keep the following principles in mind when leading God's people in worship.

First, remember that God doesn't need our music—he wants our hearts. Teach people how to worship with sincere and honest motives (Col. 3:17). People can always spot a fake. If you practice genuine worship in front of people, they will follow.

Second, God called you to minister to those who are in your congregation—not the church down the street. Accept that as your first calling. It really isn't important what the people at the church down the street think about you and your worship ministry. It is important what God thinks about you and your faithfulness. It is important that you meet the needs of your people.

Third, you cannot afford to get sidetracked in controversy. God wants you to direct your hearts and lead his people to his throne in worship. As we have seen in church history, people have always debated the do's and don'ts of worship. You need to keep your focus on leading God's people in worship.

Fourth, teach people the joy of singing to the Lord not just singing about him. God is seeking worshipers. Lead people in singing to the Lord.

Fifth, you cannot afford to discard the old; you must learn from the past. You cannot, you must not, do away with the traditions of the past just because you have found a new way to do something. Tread carefully when making changes. Make sure your decisions are guided by the Holy Spirit.

Sixth, always remember you are building people—building a future for someone else, building spiritual soldiers, building relationships, building worship leaders, building a heritage, building a work unto the Lord.

Seventh, do more than provide an adequate *worship ministry.* Give people your very best. God commands the best of our labor. God's people deserve no less.

The Dynamics of Serving and Worship

And whatsoever ye do, do it heartily, as to the Lord, and not unto men.

Colossians 3:23 KJV

It was a sweltering June Sunday in the southern flatlands of Georgia. The teenagers of my church met for a final Sunday afternoon choir rehearsal. The fifty-voice group had completed its first tour and now was ready to present the program to friends, relatives, and neighbors. The tour had been a testimony of grace. The group visited teenagers, sang in retirement homes, and helped at a country church during Vacation Bible School. Several young people committed themselves to full-time Christian ministry, and all of us experienced God in a new, fresh, and dynamic way. The teens learned an important lesson about worship while serving.

One choir member especially learned this lesson. His name was Mike, and he loved the Lord with all his heart. He followed me around to the radio station, on hospital visitation, to the mall. He was always willing to help, and he constantly talked about the Lord. He asked questions about worship and serving. Once he asked about God's call on a minister of music. At the age of fifteen he was already sensitive to the Holy Spirit and the need to have a servant's heart. He loved serving others, and he had a heart for God. Mike became a fellow servant in ministry.

The Bible has much to say about serving, giving, and doing unto the Lord. Ephesians admonishes us to serve according to our gifts (Eph. 4:1–16). First and Second Corinthians encourage us to serve one another with love for the Lord and for one another (1 Corinthians 13; 2 Cor. 5:11–21; 8:1–9). First and Second Thessalonians and Titus admonish us to serve until he comes (1 Thess. 4:1–18; 2 Thess. 2:1–16; Titus 2:11–15). The New Testament rendering for *serving* or *service* is "ministry." Whether one is on the paid staff of a church or serves as an unpaid worship leader, that person is ministering in music, serving through music. We minister (serve) when we take the concepts of worship from the textbook and to the congregation.

Worship through Service

In Philippians 2, we learn about one of the apostle Paul's fellow servants, Epaphroditus. Epaphroditus understood the principle that ministry is unto the Lord. He understood that worship is a lifestyle that begins with worship to the Lord and concludes with service to and with fellow servants. Paul commends Epaphroditus as one who ministered to his needs (Phil. 2:25). *Ministered* in this passage is the same word used for ministry in the temple by the high priest. It implies much sacredness. The implication is that serving God's people and ministry unto the Lord are one and the same. We have a responsibility to serve God's people with an attitude of love coupled with actions that illustrate genuine love of God as Lord. How does one learn to do this kind of service? How can one apply the principles gleaned from the life of Epaphroditus in Philippians 2:25 to concepts of corporate worship? *First, to understand how to worship through serving, one should practice building relationships.* Many a foolish musician, worship leader, pastor, and teacher has stepped on feelings, used friendships, taken advantage of others, and generally ignored relationships in an effort to get ahead—only to be left at the end of life with missed opportunities, hurt feelings, angry colleagues, and disappointed partners. Your relationships—with God, family members, other believers, and those in your work community—make the difference in successful long-term corporate worship leading. Epaphroditus apparently understood the importance of building relationships.

Second, recognize the need to serve. Epaphroditus understood his mandate to serve. The Bible says that "he longs for all of you." He knew the Philippian brothers and sisters. He was genuine in his interest in their lives. He apparently worried about their needs and made a number of efforts to minister to them, in spite of great hardship.

Third, one must be teachable in order to worship through service. Epaphroditus was teachable. Paul had so ingrained in Epaphroditus the concept of working with people as co-laborers that the philosophy was practiced in Philippi as Epaphroditus ministered to his brothers and sisters in need.

The apostle Paul was apparently a great supervisor to Epaphroditus. Paul understood the importance of managing human resources as he taught Epaphroditus how to labor with him in ministry. The fact that Paul mentored Epaphroditus is most significant. It illustrates the concept of a team ministry. Philippians 2:25–28 illustrates the importance of Epaphroditus laboring with Paul not for Paul. The moment Epaphroditus would have begun working for Paul or for Paul's approval, he would have been living in the fear of man. Many a worship leader, pastor, minister of music, Christian worker, and fellow believer lives in the fear of man. Work is done for God rather than unto God. A person living in the fear of man finds himself doing ministry that is acceptable on the basis of another person's approval. Epaphroditus was free of the fear of man.

Fourth, partnerships are important when serving. Paul and Epaphroditus worked together as a team. Jesus sent people out in pairs to preach. God answers prayer when two or three join together. Two are to go to a brother when there has been a wrong. Partnerships are essential to the success of any ministry. When people work together, those involved have a sense of ownership in the task. A closer look reveals the heart of this partnership. Paul calls Epaphroditus *brother* (Phil. 2:25). The word *brother* means to come from the same womb, to have the same origin, to be at the same level. Epaphroditus is referred to as a companion in labor.

This issue of partnership in ministry is crucial to successful leadership. Equally important is the need for partnership with the people being served. Partnership in worship begins with the pastor and includes the staff, the various boards, and the congregation. The people at Philippi were fellow soldiers, co-campaigners, associates in work, companions in labor, co-laborers, helpers, and work fellows. There was a common bond—a relationship—between Paul and Epaphroditus that carried over into their relationships with the people they served. Epaphroditus had a genuine love for his people, and they rejoiced when they saw him and received him with gladness.

The fifth characteristic of worship and service is an unselfish spirit. Epaphroditus did not expect anything in return for his labor. He was a true servant. A servant always remains a servant. He never feels sorry for himself, taken advantage of, stepped on, or deemed unimportant. He is not above doing the lowest task. Why? Because he is a servant. Epaphroditus did not minister because he expected anything in return. He ministered to the Christians because he genuinely loved them and cared about their every need.

Why should we be surprised? Epaphroditus learned it well. Paul, his mentor, was even willing to delay his own departure to heaven if it better served the needs of those at Philippi: "I am torn between the two: I desire to depart and be with Christ, which is better by far; but it is more necessary for you that I remain in the body" (Phil. 1:23–24).

Epaphroditus's motive reflects a genuine concern for those with whom he worked in spirit and in deed. In Philippians 2:26, we see that he longed after them. Perhaps this illustrates his unselfish, unwavering, faithful, and loyal philosophy of ministry: *He served as unto the Lord.*

It was because of a servant's heart that Epaphroditus was mentored by one of the Bible's great scholars, missionaries, and teachers. He was accepted as a coworker and fellow servant because his heart was prone to ministry. He was revered as a companion in labor by practicing servanthood in his daily life. He genuinely loved and worked among his people, and they received him with gladness. The Bible says that Epaphroditus had the reputation of thinking about others first (Phil. 2:30). He loved all the brethren at Philippi with an intense, faithful love even to the point that he risked his life to see their needs supplied. He even worried about their concern over him during a time of sickness. He did not play favorites or minister only to those closest to his age or cultural mind-set. He ministered to (served) all God's people.

The scope of worship through serving involves more than getting an immediate task completed. It is a lifestyle, a mind-set, a guiding compass, a philosophy, a shared vision, and a heart attitude. We worship the Lord as we serve one another.

I've been around many a musician who was too arrogant, conceited, and self-righteous to be used by God for ministry. Their opinions of themselves were too lofty for effective ministry. They forgot the reason for performing sacred music. Worship leaders, ministers of music, pastors, church musicians, sound technicians, and anyone involved in leading corporate worship must approach ministry with a servant's heart. God wants servants. He wants men and women willing to give, motivated by a genuine love for the Master. It is when our love for God drives us to a position of service that involves every aspect of human life that we can effectively worship.

The Principles of Worship through Service

Service is the outward evidence of our worshiping hearts—privately and collectively. When we lead people in worship, we lead them through the process of ministering to the Lord. Each time we meet to sing, pray, read Scripture, and share the wonders of God with one another, we accept the responsibility of being associates in ministry—partners in serving one another while we worship. So what have we learned from our study of Epaphroditus that will help us develop a lifestyle of worship through service?

First, we need to understand the importance of relationships—with God, family, coworkers, and friends.

Second, we should minister with people and not for people. We will not have a long-term ministry if our concept is to minister for people's approval.

Third, we need to practice ministry in our daily living—with our family, our spouses, our children, our coworkers.

Fourth, worship through service requires that we have a genuine concern for those with whom we work and minister—at work, at home, at church.

Fifth, genuine worship through service will enable us to look at those with whom we minister as brothers in Christ and companions in ministry.

Sixth, to be successful at worship through service we must reflect a philosophy of ministry that is unselfish, grounded in faith, and all inclusive.

Seventh, key to successful worship-service is the ability to serve people as unto the Lord.

Eighth is the principle of seeing ministry as a partnership privilege.

Ninth, one must be teachable to worship through service.

Finally, to be equipped as worshipers who serve, we must capture the vision to do, learn, work, and witness with hearts compelled by love and worship of the living Lord.

It has been nearly twenty years since I led that youth choir in Georgia. Those teenagers are all grown now. Some went on to college, others joined the armed services, one or two left home in rebellion, but most are still in the church serving the Lord, rearing their families, and watching their children sing unto the Lord.

And Mike, well Mike has never lost his servant's heart. He was a football player in high school. He turned down scholarships and went to Bible college. He returned home, went on to graduate school, and now is a CPA. He's married and has children of his own. He is still a servant. He still loves helping God's people do God's work. And he's never lost sight of the importance of knowing God. And, by the way, he still sings in the choir. Maybe in one way Mike is like Epaphroditus. He learned early that acceptable service to God is an outgrowth of worship of God.

The Dynamics of Practical Worship

> May the favor of the Lord our God rest upon us;
> establish the work of our hands for us—
> yes, establish the work of our hands.
>
> Psalm 90:17

Second Chronicles 6:40–41 has always intrigued me. Here, in the middle of this prayer by King Solomon, God is petitioned to take his rest. God rest? Yes, that is what Solomon asks God to do. He says, "Take your rest."

In context, this must be one of the most profound offerings of praise. Solomon finished the awesome task of building the temple, the primary purpose of which was to provide a dwelling place for God. Solomon's prayer is a final act of praise. He invites God to "come and rest" in the dwelling place set aside as the residence for the Lord of Lords. Solomon was in effect saying, "God, come and abide where you belong."

I believe that God was already perfecting praise in Solomon's heart by the time the King of Israel invited God to "take his resting place." Capture the picture of 2 Chronicles 5:11–14. Solomon calls all the leaders from the tribe of Levi to join together in bringing the ark of the covenant to the temple. He prepares for the dedication of the temple and recognizes that the temple was built as a house of praise. Why? It is the dwelling place of God.

Each group or division from the tribe of Levi is called on to participate in this grand praise service. God's name is praised, and he honors their commitment to praise by filling the room with his presence. God comes down and visits. So intense is his glory and presence that the preachers have to stop ministering to God's people.

Solomon approaches the throne of God with confidence and faith when he begins the prayer in 2 Chronicles 6 because he is filled with an understanding of God. Solomon experiences the presence of God and witnesses the power and the presentation of divine praise. When God is praised, he blesses his people with his presence. Perhaps this experience forever changed Solomon's perspective on praise.

I find it remarkable that all the worship leaders and musicians and preachers were able to get along. The Bible says they worshiped *together,* with one voice. That means they worked in one accord, praised God with one heart and mind, and as a result, God sent his blessings. By the time Solomon gets to 2 Chronicles 6:40–41, he is captured by the wonder and presence of God. Solomon's praise is a practical response to being in the presence of Jehovah.

Making Praise Practical

So how does our praise become practical? How do we apply the principles in these two passages to our lives so that our corporate worship is both practical and dynamic? How do we perfect and develop a pattern for praise?

Listed below are seven ways that our corporate praise can be made practical. Some of the principles come from the passages in 2 Chronicles 5 and 6. Other principles have been taken from my own personal time with God, my system for planning private worship, and the patterns I use in crafting corporate worship.

The first principle for making our praise practical is to pray praise. Couched in the middle of this historical record of Solomon's dedication of the temple is an incredible prayer of praise. Solomon praised God for being God. He bragged about God. He thanked him for his care and love through the generations.

I suggest that if we want God to come and bless our worship services, we need to begin by praising God for being God. Praise him for his majesty. Pray for God to send his power on you as offerings of worship are presented in his name. Ask him to give you power to lead worship. Pray that you will clearly present Jesus as the joy of salvation and the only way to God. Ask God to bless your worship with the presence of his Holy Spirit. Ask God to send his Spirit as Jehovah-Shalom, the God of peace, to breathe his sweet breath across the hearts of those in your congregation who have serious emotional needs. Tell God that you love him. Ask him to come and join with the brethren as you sing praise to God (Heb. 2:11–12). Pray that God will be blessed and pleased by your worship.

The second principle for making praise practical is preparation. It took an incredible amount of work on Solomon's part to make the necessary preparations for worship. In Solomon's case, he built a new temple. Primary to the success of corporate worship is preparation. Prepare yourself and God's people to worship. In so doing, prepare for the expected and expect the unexpected. Such preparation also involves considering the purpose of the service. Each service has a different purpose resulting in a different dynamic. Ask yourself if you are preparing for a regular weekly service, a special praise service, a seeker-sensitive or evangelistic meeting, or some type of special event—

communion, baptism, baby dedication, and so on. Then plan accordingly.

The third principle for making praise practical is planning. I like to see my role in organizing and worship planning as similar to that of a carpenter gathering tools, laying out building materials in an orderly fashion, studying the blueprint, and systematically constructing a building. Keyboards, projectors, musicians, various musical instruments, music, hymnals, chorus books, lighting, and sound equipment are my tools. My materials are themes, ideas, Scripture, drama, songs, and various traditions. The materials are brought to life by people using the tools for the kingdom of God.

In developing a worship service, I find it practical to work within the framework of a theme. Often, I make an outline of what I want to communicate in a particular service. I use the outline as a starting place for constructing a service. Many pastors plan their sermon topics well in advance, thus allowing the worship leader to follow some type of theme.

After determining the theme, I seek to find out the total length of the program. How long is the service from beginning to end? How long is the worship portion of the service? The length of service will often help me decide how many non-musical elements should be included. Non-musical elements include Scripture, drama, responsive readings, testimonies, faith stories, prayer, and the sermon.

The fourth way to make praise practical is by carefully paying attention to the pacing of a service. Pacing is the tempo or speed at which worship moves from song to Scripture to prayer to song in a service. Remember, we want to structure our worship so that all the attention and the glory goes to the Lord. Pacing is important because it has a great deal to do with the emotional success of a service. In my opinion, pacing is more important to the ministry of worship than anything except prayer and the work of the Holy

Spirit. The idea is to have one seamless flow from the beginning to the end of a service.

The general overriding rule for pacing is to make the changes and shifts from one section of the service to the next as smoothly and consistently as possible. Here are three things to consider when crafting the pacing of a service:

1. The choice of tempo in songs is important to the emotional drama of a worship service. We are emotional creatures, and it takes some time for us to adjust to songs that suddenly change in tempo. I choose to use faster songs first that may be followed by slower songs.
2. Be conscious of the style of music being used in worship. If your congregational worship includes the use of both worship and praise choruses and traditional hymns, move from the contemporary, up-tempo songs to the more traditional. Rarely do I move from more traditional to high-energy contemporary songs.
3. Make sure to interweave non-musical worship events and/or activities with the musical elements. In most evangelical churches, contemporary or traditional, services are divided and broken up into sections. Use Scripture and drama as transitional material between slower and faster songs, to move into the sermon, or to move into a video presentation or something special. Follow Scripture and prayer with a song of commitment or inspiration.

The fifth principle for making praise practical involves practicing praise. I'm referring here to the rehearsal of the service. Individually, I rehearse the entire service. After I have planned an order of service, secured each person to participate in the worship ministry, chosen each Scripture passage, selected each song, and assigned each prayer, I literally practice the order of worship—from beginning to end. I sing each song, read aloud each Scripture passage, and pray each prayer. I find that whenever I practice worship privately, I'm ready to lead it publicly.

I have the joyous opportunity of leading worship at Olive Baptist Church in Pensacola, Florida. My pastor, Dr. Ted Traylor, has the unusual ability to keep worship flowing from song to prayer, prayer to Scripture reading, Scripture reading back to song, song to giving, and so forth. Sharing the platform with him is much like being on a track and field relay team and handing the baton off to the next runner. The difference is that we are handing off the baton of praise. Dr. Traylor often sets the stage for continual worship by thematically tailoring his prayer to the text of the next song. Rarely do we plan these transitions ahead of time. I simply tell him we need a prayer or hand him a Scripture passage to read. He always captures the "spirit of the moment." Sometimes the flow between the two of us is so smooth that one would think we rehearse together or that my pastor plans the service for me—songs and all.

Recently, after about ten or twelve of these kinds of services, my curiosity got the best of me and I asked Dr. Traylor how he is able to lead these aspects of worship so smoothly.

"Well," he said, "I practice it, Vernon. I practice your worship services."

I found out that Dr. Traylor practices every service I create for Olive Baptist Church. On Saturday night, during his preparation time for the Sunday service, Dr. Traylor takes the printed order of worship in one hand, a hymnal in the other, and practices the service from beginning to end. He sings every song, prays every prayer, reads every Scripture passage, and preaches every point—in the privacy of his own study. He practices worship.

It is also important to practice praise as a group. The praise team, choir, soloists, and members of the drama team all need to practice the worship service together. Practice the transitions, key changes, and order of worship. In addition to practicing notes and rhythms, the entire team should practice worship.

The sixth principle for making praise practical involves people. The Holy Spirit calls people to worship God in spirit and in truth. He gives men and women gifts so that they can lead people in worship. Remember that your musicians are fellow ministers. They are called by God to lead the body of Christ in worship. Crucial to the success of any worship ministry is the relationship a worship pastor has with the other worship participants. Top priority must be given to building dynamic relationships with fellow musicians and worshipers.

The seventh and final principle for making praise practical involves praise itself. "By him therefore let us offer the sacrifice of praise to God continually, that is, the fruit of our lips giving thanks to his name" (Heb. 13:15 KJV). Do it. Praise God with all your heart. Lead God's people to praise God. As you lead corporate worship, limit your talking by planning well in advance what you are going to say. Remember to keep the pacing of the service consistent. Do not waste time. Finally, leave the results up to the Holy Spirit. He will do the job of bringing people to the throne room in worship much better than any of us.

Corporate Worship Begins in the Heart

On several occasions in this book, I emphasized the principle of practicing praise and worship privately before ever attempting to lead corporate worship. The resources needed for corporate praise are drawn from the presence of Jesus in our hearts. It is the indwelling power of the Holy Spirit that enables us to find ways to engage others in corporate worship. As we praise and worship him privately, he makes us more and more aware of his presence in our lives. He teaches us to know his presence. And his sweet spirit grants the discernment to enjoy his presence.

How does one prepare privately for public praise? First, at the beginning of the day, our lips should speak praise to God. Throughout the business of the day, our lives should explode with gratitude and praise. And when laying our heads down on our pillows at night, we should utter praise.

Second, at the risk of sounding repetitive, praise must be constantly on our lips. Praise and worship should not be reserved for corporate gatherings. Praising God needs to become a way of life.

Third, set aside special times and places to praise God. Practice praising him in your car on the way to work. Praise him when taking a shower in the morning. My wife enjoys spending time with God in the patio room of our house as she looks across the grass to the beauty of God's creation.

Fourth, prepare your heart for praise by seeking God's forgiveness of sin. Ask God to make you aware of any sin in your life. Ask him to help you be sensitive to the Holy Spirit and to remove from your heart any predisposition to sin.

Fifth, pace your private time with God by moving from exaltation to adoration, celebration to surrender, and commendation to commitment. I ask God to intercede on behalf of my friends or to meet special needs in my life only after I have first praised and worshiped him for who he is.

Sixth, seek new and meaningful ways to practice praise. Sing to God. Clap your hands to the Lord. Quote promises from Scripture. Thank him for keeping his word. Keep a written record of your praise and petitions. Occasionally, read your record, noting the answered prayers in your life.

Seventh, as you practice praising God in private, he will stir within your soul the desire to praise him in public. The more you praise, the more you will want to encourage other people to praise him too.

I've shared practical principles of corporate worship in this chapter. Many of these principles are gleaned from the worship practices of King Solomon. Remember, Solomon built and prepared the temple as a dwelling place for God. The Bible records how the presence of God filled the temple (2 Chron. 5:11–14). God no longer dwells in a physical temple. Rather, he chooses to dwell in our hearts when we trust him as Lord and Savior. Just as Solomon prepared the physical temple for worship of Jehovah, we need to prepare our spiritual temple (our hearts) for corporate worship. We need to prepare our hearts to enjoy his presence. As we prepare our hearts in private, God will equip us to lead his people corporately.

Epilogue

Ten Dynamic Principles for Corporate Worship

While writing this epilogue, my mother went to be with the Lord. Her death was unexpected and sudden. She went into the hospital with abdominal pains, and ten days later she was in glory. Mom was a wonderfully gifted woman with many talents and abilities. At the age of sixty-seven, for example, she went back to school and completed a degree in Christian counseling, moved from Oklahoma to her home in North Carolina, and started Hope Ministries in Kinston, North Carolina. She loved ministering to hurting people. She was a special woman. Her influence was felt up and down the eastern seaboard of North Carolina.

On one morning in February of 1996, I received an envelope from my mother. It contained her funeral plans and a list of fifteen principles for living that she wanted us children to remember. What follows are ten dynamic principles from Mom's list that can be applied to corporate worship. These principles transcend culture, style, and ecclesiastical norms and are from the heart of someone who lived a lifestyle of worship. May I suggest that these ten principles serve as a beginning place for us to develop a consensus for corporate worship?

1. Have a Passion for God!

Corporate worship is more than a neat package of songs, Scripture passages, and cultural practices. Corporate worship begins with the heart. Worship is intensely personal. Deep within each person is the desire to worship God in spirit and in truth. This kind of intense love for God involves attitudes of awe, reverence, respect, and adoration. It involves our emotions and is passionate.

2. Spend Time with God in Private Worship

Dynamic, corporate worship begins with one's private time with God. Workshops, training seminars, and college classes on worship will not do for you what time alone with God can do. The Holy Spirit is the only one who can teach you to be personal, passionate, and practical. Practice worship privately before ever doing it publicly.

3. Focus on the Purpose and Power of Corporate Worship

The purpose of corporate worship is to engage God's people in expressing love, admiration, and exaltation of Jehovah God for who he is and for what he has done. It involves facilitating opportunities of praise and worship as one group, together. God promises to inhabit the praise of his people. Only as we bless, praise, adore, and magnify his holy name does God enable us to worship in power and truth.

4. Prepare for and Practice Worship with Your Children

"From the rising of the sun to the place where it sets, the name of the LORD is to be praised" (Ps. 113:3). A person learns best how to swim when he steps into the water and starts swimming. Likewise, people learn how to worship only as they practice it. We must teach our children how to praise ("From the lips of children and infants you [God] have ordained praise" [Ps. 8:2]), or we will not have trained leaders of worship for the future. Teach worship. Live worship. Love worship. Train those around you to be worshipers.

> Love the LORD your God with all your heart and with all your soul and with all your strength. These commandments that I give you today are to be upon your hearts. Impress them on your children. Talk about them when you sit at home and when you walk along the road, when you lie down and when you get up.
>
> Deuteronomy 6:5–7

5. Don't Try to Impress God (or Anyone Else for That Matter)—Be Yourself

God doesn't need for us to prove anything. He wants us to let him use us for his kingdom's glory. The moment we seek to prove a point, promote a hidden agenda, or persuade people that our way is right for every church, God withdraws his blessings from our lives as worship leaders. Remember, God uses broken vessels for kingdom work.

6. Surround Yourself with Those Who Enjoy Corporate Worship

Paramount to successful corporate worship is the need to build the right team of worship leaders. Each person on your team needs to reflect a sincere spirit of worship. They need to demonstrate a love for God, for his people, and for your mission to worship.

7. Include All of God's People in Corporate Worship

Corporate worship that is biblical must meet the needs of the entire congregation. Corporate worship must be balanced if it is to be truly dynamic. At the heart of many worship wars is the practice of giving preference to one group's stylistic preferences at the expense of another's. If God has called you to a church as a worship pastor, he has also called you to minister to all of God's people—children, teens, young couples, singles, married adults, and senior citizens.

8. Be Willing to Change and Adapt

We live in a changing culture. Our methodology for corporate worship will, by its very nature, reflect our changing society and culture. The struggles we as worship leaders have in defining practices for corporate worship for the twenty-first century involve many of the same issues and challenges our forefathers faced. We face the same storm clouds when dealing with change. We listen to the same voices of doubt when using new methods. And I predict that Christians in the twenty-first century will face the same naysayers when meeting the diverse needs of a growing congregation.

9. Do Not Allow the Fear of Man to Control Your Motives for Corporate Worship

"Fear of man will prove to be a snare, but whoever trusts in the LORD is kept safe" (Prov. 29:25). How much does fear drive what you do as a worshiper? Fear of failure, fear of being misunderstood, fear of tomorrow, fear of others' opinions, fear of missed opportunities, fear of man. It is one thing to be sensitive to the needs of the body of Christ; it is quite another thing to make decisions out of fear. Our motives must be from an attitude of gratitude for what God is doing for us (Col. 3:16–17, 23). Our work and ministry should be unto God and not unto men (Col. 3:23).

10. Enjoy God!

Written in the back of my mother's Bible is this quote from the Westminster Catechism: "The chief end of man is to love God and to enjoy him forever." To enjoy God means to know him; spend time with him; love him; receive his forgiveness; understand his glory; rejoice in his goodness; make him known; thrill at the wonder of his presence, grace, and goodness; and worship him together.

I guess that's what I remember most about my mother's walk with God: She lived and taught worship. She loved to be where God's people were, especially as they practiced praise. As our family stood around her bed, just minutes before her home going, we sang "Blessed Assurance, Jesus Is Mine." We'd been singing choruses, hymns, and gospel songs for twenty or thirty minutes. But this time, when we got to the words "This is my story, this is my song, praising my Savior, all the day long," Mom's lips began to move in time with our singing. We sang a second verse. Again, when we got to the chorus, she sang with us. A few minutes later, she departed this world into the presence of Jesus. She marched into glory with a song of praise on her lips.

I am persuaded that when a person enjoys God in private and proclaims praise in corporate worship, our holy Lord is blessed and honored. Departing this world is not sorrow but joy. For the Christian, enjoying God, even in corporate worship, begins with a daily walk with the sovereign Lord on this earth—through lifestyle worship—and continues throughout all eternity.

Notes

Chapter 1

1. Charles C. Ryrie, *Basic Theology* (Wheaton: Victor Books, 1988), 428.
2. A. W. Tozer, *Whatever Happened to Worship?* (Camp Hill, Pa.: Christian Publications, 1985), 82, 84.
3. Ibid., 123.

Chapter 2

1. Warren W. Wiersbe, *Real Worship*, 2d ed. (Grand Rapids: Baker, 2000), 159.
2. Ibid., 112.

Chapter 3

1. A. W. Tozer, "Worship: The Normal Employment of Moral Beings," in *The Best of A. W. Tozer*, compiled by Warren W. Wiersbe (Grand Rapids: Baker, 1978), 217.

Chapter 4

1. Andrew E. Hill, *Enter His Courts with Praise* (Grand Rapids: Baker, 1993), 173.
2. Ibid., 214.
3. Ibid., 231.

Chapter 5

1. John W. Peterson, quoted in Vernon M. Whaley, "Trends in Gospel Music (1940–1960)" (Ph.D. diss., School of Music, University of Oklahoma, 1992).

Chapter 9

1. Ron Owen, *Return to Worship* (Nashville: Broadman and Holman, 1999), 48.

Chapter 10

1. Kenn Mann, "Everything I Have Is Praise" (Dayton, Ohio: Lorenz Publishing Company, 2000).

Chapter 11

1. E. M. Bounds, *Purpose in Prayer* (New York: Revell, 1929), 7–9.

Chapter 12

1. Wiersbe, *Real Worship*, 123–24.
2. Ibid., 127.

Bibliography

Best, Harold M. *Music through the Eyes of Faith.* New York: HarperSanFrancisco, 1997.

Bounds, E. M. *Purpose in Prayer.* New York: Revell, 1929.

Dawn, Marva J. *Reaching Out without Dumbing Down.* Grand Rapids: Eerdmans, 1995.

Duewel, Wesley. *Revival Fire.* Grand Rapids: Zondervan, 1995.

Eskew, Harry, and Hugh T. McElrath. *Sing with Understanding.* Nashville: Broadman, 1980.

Foster, Richard J. *Prayer.* Minneapolis: Grason, 1997.

Hill, Andrew E. *Enter His Courts with Praise.* Grand Rapids: Baker, 1993.

Hustad, Donald P. *Jubilate! Church Music in the Evangelical Tradition.* Carol Stream, Ill.: Hope Publishing, 1982.

———. *True Worship.* Carol Stream, Ill.: Hope Publishing, 1998.

Liesch, Barry. *The New Worship.* Grand Rapids: Baker, 1996.

Owens, Ron. *Return to Worship.* Nashville: Broadman and Holman, 1999.

Pratney, Winkie. *Revival: Its Principles and Personalities.* Lafayette, La.: Huntington House, 1994.

Segler, Franklin M. *Understanding, Preparing for, and Practicing Christian Worship.* 2d ed. Nashville: Broadman and Holman, 1996.

Tozer, A. W. *Whatever Happened to Worship?* Camp Hill, Pa.: Christian Publications, 1985.

Webber, Robert E., editor. *The Complete Library of Christian Worship: The Biblical Foundations of Christian Worship.* Vol. 1. Nashville: Star Song Publishing, 1993.

Whaley, Vernon M. "Trends in Gospel Music Publishing (1940–1960)." Ph.D. diss., School of Music, University of Oklahoma, 1992.

Wiersbe, Warren W. *Real Worship.* Grand Rapids: Baker, 2000.

Vernon M. Whaley is minister of music at the Olive Baptist Church in Pensacola, Florida. Dr. Whaley has distinguished himself as a teacher of church music and worship for better than twenty years. Recently serving Cedarville University as associate professor of church music and director of the Center for Church Music Ministry, he holds a Ph.D. from the University of Oklahoma and a D.Min. in church music from Luther Rice Seminary. He is the author of *Understanding Music and Worship in the Local Church* (Evangelical Training Association) and president of Integra Music Group, a music publishing company based in Brentwood, Tennessee. He has published arrangements, compositions, and orchestrations with well-known Christian music publishers, created several musicals, and edited two popular hymnals. He is a favorite of music directors, worship leaders, and pastors at conferences and music retreats. Known as a creative choral arranger, dynamic worship leader, and effective conference speaker, Dr. Whaley draws from his wealth of experience in the classroom and as a long-time minister of music to make his workshops unusually practical.